CW00961585

To get funding, be

# FUNDABLE
# & FINDABLE

## The Brand-New Way
## to Fix Your Nonprofit Fundraising

**KEVIN L. BROWN**

First published in 2025

Copyright © 2025 by Kevin L. Brown

ISBN paperback 979-8-9927881-1-2

ISBN hardback 979-8-9927881-0-5

ISBN e-book 979-8-9927881-3-6

For permission to use the Fundable/Findable Framework™ and phrases like "To get funding, be fundable and findable" or "brand first, funding second" — contact Mighty Ally.

# CONTENTS

Introduction — To get funding, be fundable and findable.

## PART ONE: BE FUNDABLE

**Theory of Change** — Fuel your fundraising, messaging, measurement, and partnerships with this brand document.

1. The Need
   A pitch without a problem is a problem.          33

2. The Work
   Complicated missions complicate fundraising.      43

3. The Results
   Sell donors on your vision, not just your cause.   59

**Strategic Plan** — Turn your theory into traction and provide proof to funders with this communications tool.

4. Team
   Fundraising starts with boards and teams, not tactics.   87

5. Priorities
   Anything is possible. Everything isn't.           99

6. Rhythms
   Goals can guide, but routines realize funding.    109

# PART TWO: BE FINDABLE

**Positioning Strategy** — Distinguish your brand and break through the noise in the minds of donors with this blueprint.

7.  Landscape
    You're competing for story instead of glory.          139

8.  Value Propositions
    Difference = donations. Emphasize it.                 149

9.  Brand Personality
    Clear brands attract. Compelling brands convert.      165

**Marketing Communications** — Amplify your story and mobilize funder audiences with these promotional practices.

10. Marketing Plan
    Brands that chase all channels chase away funding.    187

11. Messaging & Storytelling
    Give donors a story to remember, not a fact to
    memorize.                                             205

12. Writing & Thought Leadership
    Writing is a fundraising superpower.                  225

13. Visual Identity
    It's OK for nonprofits to look a little slick.        239

14. Pitch Deck
    Reject presentations, embrace conversations.         249

15. Website Strategy
    Your website is your best (or worst!) fundraiser.    259

16. Corporate Partnerships
    Corporate social responsibility: where money
    meets marketing.                                     275

# PART THREE: GET FUNDING

**Donor Acquisition** — Change how you think about nurturing and asking new donors with these brand mindsets.

17. Cultivation
    The first step in fundraising is not fundraising.          297

18. Solicitation
    You can't wake a donor who is pretending to be asleep.     309

**Donor Retention** — Manage and maintain your existing donors and resources with these brand attitudes.

19. Stewardship
    Stop stewarding, start communicating.                      329

20. Engagement
    Diversified funding is a nonprofit nemesis.                343

**CONCLUSION** — Imperfect brands make perfect sense.

**EPILOGUE** — The unrecognised force fueling the quest for a better world, by Ingrid Srinath.

**NOTES** — Everything that needs to be said has already been said.

# INTRODUCTION
## To get funding, be fundable and findable.

Too many nonprofits are unseen, unheard, and underfunded.

This realization struck me while on death row in Kenya. I was conducting field study in a dozen prisons alongside a struggling nonprofit leader. He had experienced a series of fundraising failures (including a harsh donor rejection I'll tell you about in a moment).

The nonprofit did incredible legal work with people who often had not been convicted of a crime, who often had no lawyer, and who often waited for years in crowded prison cells without a trial. These same people then learned how to defend themselves and others in court. This nonprofit created such an impact that even prison guards joined the program to legally represent those they guarded.

Inspiring.

Yet the organization barely raised enough money to stay alive, much less grow.

After listening to the remarkable work of these paralegals in prison — but seeing the *unremarkable* fundraising results — I realized something. Time and time again, nonprofit leaders are forced to fight two levels of inequality. The injustices faced by their communities. Plus, the unjust reality that most of their own organizations are stuck in the nonprofit starvation cycle.[1]

# Sound familiar?

Look at the sobering data. Only one in 1,000 nonprofits will grow beyond a small business[2] (yes, your nonprofit is a business too). Even in the United States — where philanthropic foundations have more than a trillion dollars sitting in the bank[3] — 88% of nonprofits struggle on less than $500,000 USD annually.[4] More troubling is that half of you walk a tightrope with just one month of cash reserves.[5]

It's a valley of death with nowhere to grow.

As a result, many measures such as the United Nations Sustainable Development Goals are off track or reversing.[6]

What's behind this stunted growth phenomenon? A lot of us feel like we don't have the time, team, or tools to succeed in fundraising. Especially the people closest to the very issues we're trying to solve. Like community-based organizations; leaders who are Black, Indigenous, People of Color; and local nonprofits in the Global South.

Making matters more challenging, most Executive Directors were not trained in business and leadership. Our sector is mostly run by talented specialists such as doctors, teachers, lawyers, engineers, global health experts, and scientists. In fact, 80% of growth-stage nonprofit leaders are first-time CEOs.[7]

So you're not alone in feeling overwhelmed and uncertain.

You've read all the books and blogs. Attended fundraising workshops. Hired fundraising consultants and seen countless fundraising managers come and go. You've applied for more awards, sought more funder meetings, and created more donor prospect lists.

Fundraising, fundraising, fundraising.

Yet, fundraising always feels like pitching, constantly guessing at the correct fit. You chase money. Little is known or in your control. Ultimately, your funding chase hasn't worked — at least not as well as it could. Why?

**More fundraising itself can't fix your fundraising.**

To break this nonprofit starvation cycle, we must tackle the problem differently. Of course you need to fundraise, eventually. But if your income has stalled, stop what you're doing. Stop chasing donations. Gather your leadership team and do this instead:

**To get funding, be fundable and findable.**

Being fundable means showing donors why you exist, what you do, who will do it, where you're going, how to get there, and when it will be done. That's your theory of change and your strategic plan. And *that* can fix your fundraising.

Being findable means occupying a distinct space in the minds of your ideal funders, and routinely communicating your promises to them. That's your positioning strategy and your marketing communications. And *that* can also fix your fundraising.

# Here lies the secret.

Being fundable and findable is your *brand*. Your brand consists of your theory of change, strategic plan, positioning strategy, and marketing communications. And your brand — not just more fundraising itself — can fix your fundraising.

To be clear, both brand and fundraising are critical. And inseparable. It's not about the order of *importance*, it's about the order of *operations*.

Brand is the engine; fundraising is the fuel.

Brand is aspiration; fundraising is realization.

Brand is the foundation; fundraising is the roof.

Brand is differentiation; fundraising is monetization.

Brand is the value proposition; fundraising is the value exchanged.

In other words: brand first, funding second.

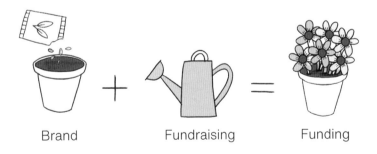

Brand          Fundraising          Funding

FIGURE 1: Brand first, funding second.

# Tough love for you brand skeptics.

Some of you despise the very idea of *brand*. The word itself gives you the capitalistic creeps.

But that sentiment isn't helping your cause. Because too many leaders wrongly think that brand is only a private-sector thing. That brand makes us compete with nonprofit peers. That brand doesn't apply to small organizations. That brand is too expensive, is all about design or creative campaigns, and shouldn't matter if the work is impactful.

Yet, none of those things is true. Here's what is:

> *"You have a brand whether you like it or not. Really, the only choice you have is how actively you want to shape and manage that brand."* — Ingrid Srinath, philanthropy geek and civil society defender (India)

If the term *brand* in this book gives you the shivers, call it *identity, clarity, unity, direction,* anything. We're talking about brand vs. brand-*ing* here. Brand is mostly strategy, much of which can be done internally with zero hard costs. So call it whatever you want. As long as you do it.

Because even a major grantmaker like Christopher Stone at Open Society Foundations says, "The brand of a nonprofit is a strategic asset central to the success of the organization itself."[8]

And remember that nonprofit leader in Kenya I told you about earlier? His harsh rejection? Well, a high-net-worth donor had just told him, "No, because your brand is shit." And this donor *wasn't* talking about the logo design or marketing collateral or campaigns. He said no to funding because the nonprofit lacked brand clarity.

Ready to move on now?

## Imagine your new future.

Let's say you've read this book, taken my advice, and built your bold brand. And you're finally fundable and findable. What does your new fundraising future look like?

In the short term, you'll see outputs like an improved theory of change, strategic plan, positioning strategy, and cohesive marketing communications — all of which will help you with early funding wins.

In the midterm, you'll feel aligned *internally*, operating with more clarity and confidence. Plus you'll feel amplified *externally*, using a louder, sharper voice to reach your audiences and spread big ideas.

Over the long term, you will maximize your funding. *Maximize* means to make as large or great as possible *and* to make the best use of. A bold brand doesn't just help you raise more money. Brand also helps you become more efficient with the funding you receive.

## How this book can help.

You're reading the only book that teaches you about the intersection of nonprofit brand and fundraising; *and* is designed for organizations at the early-stage and growth-stage; *and* is written in the Global South to include perspectives from and for international leaders, plus those in the Global North; *and* provides both conceptual insights as well as tactical tools.

> *"A book isn't about something; it's for someone."*
> *— Anjanette Harper, author (United States)*

So here's my promise to all you fellow nonprofit leaders:

**By the end of this book, you will confidently have the understanding and framework to build a clear, compelling nonprofit brand that maximizes your funding and advances social justice. In other words: you'll know how to be fundable and findable.**

The chapters are short, with subheadings, action steps, plus a summary. You can use this book as a reference when working on specific pieces of your brand. That is, *after* you've read it from beginning to end.

On that note: brands are built from the inside out. And despite what you've done before, I guarantee you've never thought about your theory of change or strategic plan like this. Not to mention, simply getting these assets on paper will fuel your fundraising immediately. It's not like Part One is just pre-work — it *is* the work. Your theory of change and strategic plan are what funders fund.

So let's get more of you to $5 million, $15 million, even $50 million in size. Because your financial resilience is the catalyst for a better world.

I promise it's not that complicated. And you can do it.

## ACTION STEP: RALLY YOUR TEAM

Here's a quick win. Tell your team that you're learning about becoming fundable and findable. Have your colleagues read this book also. But assure them: things are going to be different. Fundraising won't come first, you will finally break free from the hamster wheel, and you'll escape the nonprofit starvation cycle, once and for all.

# Why should you trust me?

I'm a social entrepreneur, too. And I've sat where you are today.

I'm a Fellow in the Acumen East Africa community, alongside hundreds of nonprofit peers. During my career, I've started or turned around four businesses: one that scaled to an international acquisition, one that failed, and two that reached solid successes.

Our own organization, Mighty Ally, is a thriving nonprofit hybrid that's funded by grantmakers like Cartier Philanthropy. (So when I use *we* or *our* language, it's because Mighty Ally is certainly a team effort.)

And we've implemented this same Fundable/Findable Framework with 340 clients in 51 countries so far, with success stories like:

- $5.5M in gifts plus a 2,110% spike in donations for Justice Defenders (East Africa)

- $750k in two impact investment rounds with Vega Coffee (Colombia and Nicaragua)

- $2M Skoll Award win in 2025 for Community Health Impact Coalition (international)

- 1,357% boom in social media engagements after a month with STiR Education (India)

- $6.7M in increased revenue for Lwala Community Alliance (United States and Kenya)

- 1.5 times the engagement ROI within six months for Humanity Crew (the Middle East)

Of course, many factors contributed to all these wins. But each organization would tell you: brand was certainly *a* factor.

Don't be fooled. The framework in this book isn't solely for big organizations — many of our clients are small nonprofits. And brand transformation doesn't always require a massive consulting engagement. Just take this praise from a funder of grassroots nonprofit leaders:

> *"I am in awe of Kevin's ability to simplify what could potentially be complex concepts, and to translate them into practical actions for emerging nonprofits. We couldn't have picked a better brand specialist to reignite our partners' missions, inspire their brands, and reinvigorate their fundraising." — Sibongile Khumalo, institutional funder (South Africa)*

That testimonial came after a one-hour keynote speech. So if this Fundable/Findable Framework can *reignite*, *inspire*, and *reinvigorate* fundraising in a single talk, the lessons in this book will do even better.

I'll also do my best to bring you the perspectives of a funder. As I'm on the advisory board of two institutional donors: Greenwood Place in England and Roddenberry Foundation in the United States.

Finally, this work is my personal purpose. I'm the proud father of three girls, from China and Uganda, born into the orphan crisis. And I'm motivated by an urgent vision where nobody faces poverty and injustice like my daughters once did. That's why I've prioritized living in three different economic contexts on three continents — growing up in America (high-income), moving to Uganda (low-income) for four years, and spending the past five years in South Africa, Mauritius, and Malaysia (middle-income).

So, after my LinkedIn content exploded from 2,800 to 70,000 followers in two years, it was clear: many nonprofit leaders crave this brand-new way to fix their fundraising. Once I announced my book and got 273 people in 49 countries to sign up as beta readers, it was time to write.

## A final note: this is *not* a fundraising book.

If you thought you needed to learn about fundraising, let me help you see that raising money is the outcome of having a great brand and great communications.

So I won't teach you how to create prospect lists, or conduct donor outreach, or write grant applications. And I won't cover topics like donor identification and qualification, as you'll *not* see in Part

Three: Get Funding. Because countless books already cover those traditional fundraising topics.

But remember, if you put in the real work to *be fundable* and *be findable*, you'll have every opportunity to *get funding*.

And this work together begins by developing your theory of change, which is our starting point in Part One: Be Fundable.

---

## ACTION STEP: BLOCK YOUR TIME

Put 20 minutes per day on your calendar for the next 20 days. Each morning, commit to reading a single chapter of this book for 10 minutes. And then start to implement the findings for another 10 minutes to get the ball rolling. That's all it will take to see progress.

---

# Summary.

1. More fundraising itself can't fix your fundraising. To get funding, be fundable and findable.

2. You have a brand, whether you like it or not. And raising lots of money is the outcome of having a great brand and great communications.

3. Nonprofits don't need much budget to build a bold brand. Most of brand building is strategy, not brand-*ing* (which is largely design).

4. By the end of this book, you will have the understanding and the Fundable/Findable Framework to build a clear, compelling nonprofit brand that maximizes your funding.

5. This Fundable/Findable Framework is just as applicable for the growth-stage nonprofits we at Mighty Ally consult with deeply, as it is for the early-stage organizations we train in a group setting through funder portfolios, as it is for anyone navigating our self-paced, online course.

# PART ONE:
# BE FUNDABLE

Showing donors why you exist,
what you do, who will do it,
where you're going, how to get there,
and when it will be done.

# THEORY OF CHANGE
Fuel your fundraising, messaging, measurement, and partnerships with this brand document.

Bangladesh had just won its independence. But in March 1972, the battle to rebuild had only begun. Famine loomed and disease spread and millions of people were left in poverty.

In these darkest hours, Fazle Hasan Abed — a former Shell executive turned humanitarian — took a defiant stand. Abed's vision went beyond immediate food and shelter. He dreamed of lasting change for his new country. That moment sparked his creation of the Bangladesh Rehabilitation Assistance Committee (BRAC), which would go on to become the world's largest NGO.

Over the years, however, BRAC's theory of change has stayed focused on addressing the underlying causes of poverty and believing that people can transform their own lives if given the right tools. And the organization's significant growth is a testament to how a well-constructed theory of change can evolve to meet diverse challenges, while staying true to its core.

Not all of you want or need to become an international NGO like BRAC. But just think — BRAC started out small just like the rest of us.

So the point remains. Step one in being fundable is developing your theory of change, like BRAC did decades ago. More than just a brand document, it's your nonprofit's most important tool for creating sustained impact, enhancing your marketing communications, and raising money.

But developing one can be daunting, as there's no standard format. Many theories of change are so abstract — charts, arrows, graphs, assumptions — that they're impossible to put into action. And impossible to communicate clearly to donors. Worse, some philanthropic foundations require a theory of change to be crafted within their proprietary (sometimes arbitrary) parameters. Even popular concepts, such as the logic model, have various versions.

Our Mighty Ally clients often feel like they're grasping at straws when trying to articulate their ideal impact. And others say they're too busy doing the work to stop and put that very work down on paper. That's why many organizations stop after creating a mission and a vision — two of *many* necessary elements.

But before you can create your impact — or create your brand or fundraising appeals — you must document the change you wish to see in the world.

In this section, you'll learn more about a theory of change: **what it is, why it matters,** and **how to create one.** Then, you'll fully unpack the three main parts of a theory of change in Chapters 1, 2, and 3.

Let's dive in.

# What it is.

Harvard scholar Carol Weiss — who popularized the term *theory of change*[1] — says it's a way to describe the mini-steps that lead to the long-term goal. Plus the connections between program activities and outcomes that occur along the way. The theory of change was developed decades ago to solve a common challenge: it was difficult to fund or evaluate a particular project or organization when it wasn't clear exactly what the program had set out to do in the first place.

Today, here's a more straightforward way to define a theory of change:

**Why** you exist.

**What** you do.

**Where** you're going.

To think of this process visually and metaphorically, imagine that every nonprofit is climbing a mountain. You know **why** you're climbing the mountain (that's your *reason* for doing so or *the need*). Then you pick **where** you're going and the summit you're trying to reach (your *vision* or *the results* you want to see). And finally, you determine **what** route you will take up the mountain (your *mission* or *the work* you do).

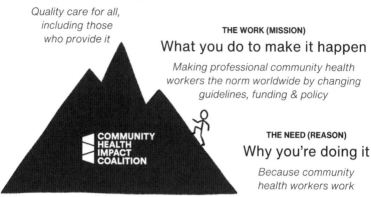

**THE RESULTS (VISION)**
Where you want to go

*Quality care for all,
including those
who provide it*

**THE WORK (MISSION)**
What you do to make it happen

*Making professional community health
workers the norm worldwide by changing
guidelines, funding & policy*

**THE NEED (REASON)**
Why you're doing it

*Because community
health workers work*

COMMUNITY
HEALTH
IMPACT
COALITION

FIGURE 2: CHIC's reason, mission, and vision.
Image adapted from Brand the Change.[2]

## CLIENT EXAMPLE: COMMUNITY HEALTH IMPACT COALITION

When we first met this client, they had a reasonably clear mission but no reason for being or a vision statement. So, their fundraising story was incomplete. But after using this climb model, they can now communicate why they exist, what they do, and where they want to go. And if you look at their brand materials (like their website), you'll see these statements from their theory of change messaged clearly and consistently everywhere.

So if you do nothing else, your theory of change should at least list your reason, mission, and vision. Those are, by far, the three most critical components for impact — and for your upcoming fundraising communications as well. In fact, my Founding Partner Eve Wanjiru leads a free Mighty Ally short course on Acumen Academy called *Theory of Change for Brand Communications*.[3] And it only covers these three elements, for simplicity.

As a program or organization grows and develops, so does its theory of change. This document is merely a snapshot of your ambition at one point in time. Meaning that a theory of change is both a living document and a work in progress — a draft that you can refine as the conditions on the ground change (or at least revisit once a year during annual planning).

Your theory of change should be a telescope. Not a magnifying glass. Think of it as a target. Not a mirror. It's a launchpad for moonshots. Not a landing strip for usual operations.

## Why it matters: maximized funding.

Here's the deal: a theory of change is what you're selling. It's what you're communicating in your brand. So unless you're a social enterprise with a tangible product that a customer is buying, your theory of change is actually what donors are investing in.

This magical document can help you:

- Raise money

- Inform staffing

- Motivate teams

- Clarify messaging

- Fine-tune programs

- Generate partnerships

- Improve measurement

- Develop a strategic plan

Further, driving impact often requires saying *no* more than saying *yes*, in order to focus. And that takes courage. This theory of change process and document will aid in that courageous focus.

Even in the social sector — where meaning and motivation abound — teams need to rally around a singular greater ambition. If you set a clear theory of change, you will ultimately find the right strategic plan (covered in the next section). But no strategic plan will save you if you don't have a clear theory of change.

So nonprofit leaders: use your theory of change to sketch the various routes to impact, communicate a vision, and fuel your fundraising. Because this theory is the compelling dream of what your brand — and the world — could be.

Theorize, then mobilize. Concept to reality.

> *"A good theory of change doesn't simply reflect what an organization is already doing; rather, it articulates what the organization wants to be held accountable for, and works backward to identify necessary activities, strategies, resources, capabilities, culture, and so on. If your theory of change work hasn't led you to propose any changes to these elements, you probably haven't taken a hard enough look."* — Matthew Forti, nonprofit leader (United States)

# How to create your theory of change.

You can think of your theory of change in three big parts: the need, the work, and the results. This proprietary tool we created at Mighty Ally takes inspiration ranging from modern approaches, such as the Impact Management Project and Mulago Foundation's Design Iteration Format, to traditional frameworks like the logic model.

Here's the high-level summary:

**The need:** In Chapter 1 you will articulate the problem you're trying to solve, the people you serve, and the reason behind your work.

**The work:** In Chapter 2 you'll define your inputs, interventions, partners, behaviors, big idea, and mission.

**The results:** In Chapter 3 you can document your pathway, outputs, short-term outcome, long-term outcomes, 10-year target, and vision.

And you should be able to capture the highlights of your entire theory of change in a single-page blueprint, like Figure 3.

It becomes a powerful tool to flash on screen during a donor meeting. (This blueprint is exactly what I use myself in business development conversations.)

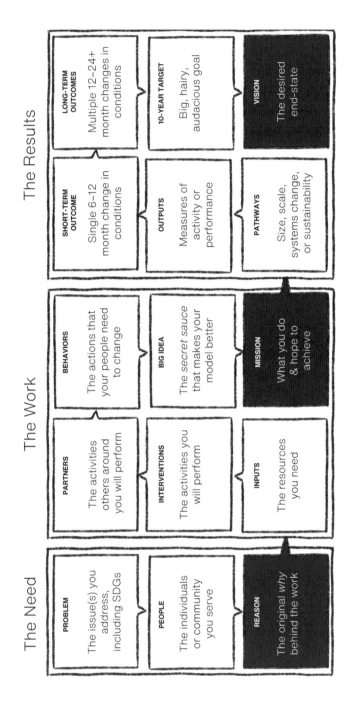

The Need

The Work

The Results

**PROBLEM**
The issue(s) you address, including SDGs

**PEOPLE**
The individuals or community you serve

**REASON**
The original *why* behind the work

**PARTNERS**
The activities others around you will perform

**INTERVENTIONS**
The activities you will perform

**INPUTS**
The resources you need

**BEHAVIORS**
The actions that your people need to change

**BIG IDEA**
The *secret sauce* that makes your model better

**MISSION**
What you do & hope to achieve

**SHORT-TERM OUTCOME**
Single 6–12 month change in conditions

**OUTPUTS**
Measures of activity or performance

**PATHWAYS**
Size, scale, systems change, or sustainability

**LONG-TERM OUTCOMES**
Multiple 12–24+ month changes in conditions

**10-YEAR TARGET**
Big, hairy, audacious goal

**VISION**
The desired end-state

FIGURE 3: The Mighty Ally theory of change blueprint.[4]

## Don't sweat the format.

As much as we (and our clients!) love this blueprint, use the tool or template that works well for your organization and your funders. Even if it's a rudimentary whiteboard diagram. The Design Iteration Format (DIF) I mentioned above is quite simple, and Mulago is one of the most prestigious funders out there. While its questions require great thought to answer, the DIF itself is just text on a page with an arrow or two.

So don't labor over what your theory of change looks like. Instead, sweat the thinking behind the model and the details within. Then, once it's in first-draft form on paper, spend time to ensure that it flows. From problem to vision and all points in between, ask yourself: is the logic, logical?

## You can't see your own label from inside the jar.

Thought you already knew how to communicate your ambition for change? It's OK if it becomes tougher than expected.

> *"The challenge is always how best to describe your child to other people! On the surface it looks simple. But you realize that it's not when you find yourself dealing with a plethora of questions about this child, simply because you tend to take for granted that what you know and what's in your heart are apparent to everyone." — Dr. Richard Chivaka, nonprofit CEO (South Africa)*

## You did it, now use it.

Once you have your theory of change, use it! Publish and share it widely, especially with funders. Everyone involved in your organization should be familiar with it. It's the jumping-off point for further conversations about how things are going, your strategies, and your tactics.

> *"If you were a screenwriter, you build a storyboard. If you were a teacher, you draft a curriculum plan for the year. If you were a CFO, you build a financial model that projects how you think money will flow. For impact professionals, building a theory of change can help you map out what you'll need to achieve over time in order to reach both your short-term and long-term goals."* —
> *Acumen, impact investor (global)*

That's all for the theory of change section overview. Ready to start creating yours? We continue by defining the need in Chapter 1 — which is up next — because a pitch without a problem is a problem.

# Summary.

1. A theory of change is any nonprofit's most important brand document — critical for impact, marketing communications, and fundraising.

2. A theory of change is what you're selling. It's what donors are investing in.

3. A good theory of change is a target, not a mirror.

4. Keep it simple: too many theories of change are full of arrows, assumptions, and academia.

5. Use whatever format you want, but aim for one readable page. Like the tool shared in Figure 3 above, consisting of three parts: the need, the work, and the results.

# 1. THE NEED

A pitch without a problem is a problem.

The next time a donor asks what you do, don't actually start with what you do.

Same goes for your elevator pitch, website homepage, one-sheeter, or pitch deck. Because a problem statement from your theory of change is the initial, powerful opening of all your fundraising communications.

The need is where your story begins. Movies have drama and fiction books build tension before resolution, because a gap, challenge, or demand shapes every story. Literature professor Joseph Campbell famously proved that this format has been used successfully throughout time, ranging from ancient myths to modern Bollywood scripts.

Why?

According to *Harvard Business Review*, emotions are the first screen for all information humans receive.[1] Because of the importance of emotions, people hear bad news first and loudest. This psychology dates back to cave people.

> "*Conflict creates tension and tension is an essential life attribute. Without tension there is banality, boredom, and predictability.*" — *Susan Cohen, writer (United States)*

So hit funders with the tension. In this chapter, you'll learn how to define the need, by identifying the **problem, people,** and **reason.** As always, I'll give you action steps within this (and every) chapter to help you implement the advice.

## Problem: if it's well stated, it's half solved.

Nonprofit leaders are often solution-oriented. Thus, it's hard for us to break the tendency to discuss our own work. And it feels counterintuitive to start our fundraising conversations or messaging with the problem. Especially because it's never right to dwell on the issues, cast a negative light on the communities we serve, or use deficit-based language.

All that said: never open with *we* language, because donors must understand the issue before they can care about your solution. Always lead with the problem you're solving.

Most leaders know — if only instinctually — the core social challenge they're trying to solve. The key is stating it clearly, succinctly, and articulately for the world to know it too. A tight-knit problem statement will focus your programs and external communications alike.

Many social challenges worth addressing — like poverty, hunger, and health — will likely take generations to finally solve. Meaning, there's plenty of work to be done in any single focus area. But too often, nonprofits reach beyond core causes and try to address several problems at once.

What you decide to include in your problem statement will significantly affect the rest of your theory of change. And what you communicate here will significantly affect how funders listen to the rest of your story.

## CLIENT EXAMPLE: FOOD FOR EDUCATION

*It's proven. Hungry children can't learn. They don't have the strength or attention span, and without proper nutrition a child's development lags. Decades of effort and millions of dollars have been spent, but the problem still hasn't been solved. Across Africa, effective, affordable, and sustainable school feeding programs are the exception. Not the norm. When programs do exist, they're run by outsiders who rely on bulk and processed foods. The result? Parents can't afford the lunches. National governments often have good intentions, but they need support to deliver nutritious programs at scale. Consequently, in a place like Kenya, 80% of children in public primary schools have no access to a nutritious school meal.*

---

On the surface, our client had a simple problem: school meals. But the typical "hungry kids" message misses much of the nuance. Especially since Food for Education was aiming to scale significantly beyond its own direct implementation — by first proving and then refining a model that was strong enough, cheap enough, and context-specific enough to be the model that scales throughout Africa. So while we opened the problem statement centered on the child, we quickly expanded into the effects on parents, governments, and the system at large. All that in just 29 seconds of reading time and at a seventh-grade reading level.

## ACTION STEP: DEFINE THE PROBLEM

Describe the key social challenge your work addresses. Why is this a problem, and why should others take notice?

- Keep it concise! 3–5 bullet points at first.
- Include a major data point (or two!) to reinforce the need.
- If you want, you can also align your statement with one or two of the UN Sustainable Development Goals.
- Then craft it into a full paragraph of a few sentences.
- Remember, this statement is not about you at all!

Of all the action steps in this book, your problem statement will take a bit more time to get right.

---

The entire problem statement paragraph from your theory of change will be helpful in some places. Like when you're copying and pasting into a funding application. Or maybe in a more extended copy block on a website subpage.

But in many settings, you'll need a much shorter soundbite version. Because you'll have to hook your audience immediately. Or they're lost.

Leaders often say, "There's no way we can dumb down this issue to one or two sentences. It's complex and interconnected!" Of course that's true. In fact, many of these problems have deep, tangled roots in colonialism. So this stuff goes way back. Then there's ongoing greed, corruption, apathy, and countless other issues making society's problems worse.

But you don't have to cover it all, right away. Instead, think of this short soundbite as just the tip of an iceberg. You're only sharing the 10% above water, so to speak. Then your audience can ask if they want to hear about the other 90% below the surface.

Still uncomfortable cutting out so much background information? Here's a messaging trick. Start with your problem soundbite, then say, "I'm happy to share more about the problem we're tackling. But first, I'll tell you about our solution." This approach lets you stay brief, indicates you have much more knowledge on the topic, and invites friendly collaboration.

Give it a try.

Now that you've determined your soundbite to hook audiences, use it. Everywhere! It's no exaggeration to say there's not a single piece of fundraising communications that wouldn't benefit from using problem language. For example, explain the problem on your website — ideally, the homepage header area — and weave it into materials like pitch decks.

# People: who do you serve?

Talking about the problem is never enough. You need to pinpoint *who* within that problem you're serving. Like if the problem is healthcare, are you working with children? Moms? Families? The elderly? Communities? Governments? Rural or urban? Local or national? You get the point. With limited resources, your impact depends on focus. So, who gets the priority?

Choose wisely.

Whether you call them beneficiaries, clients, participants, or something else (and whether they're co-creators in your mission or recipients of aid) you must be clear.

They're people with real needs and real stories — not just statistics. Don't just label them — *understand* them. Because their story is your story. Make sure you're telling it right.

**CLIENT EXAMPLE: REACH FOR CHANGE**

*We support early-stage, local social entrepreneurs in Europe and Africa that positively impact the lives of children and youth.*

---

This might seem like a simple sentence, but countless decisions lie within it. In the process of crafting their problem, we asked: Is it aimed at early-stage entrepreneurs or perhaps all of them? Are they local or expat-led? Is it targeted at social entrepreneurship the field, social enterprise the organization, or social entrepreneurs themselves as people? Geographically, where does the work begin and end? And finally, this sentence acknowledges that while Reach for Change doesn't itself work with children and youth, all their entrepreneurs must.

**ACTION STEP: NAME THE PEOPLE**

Think of the group(s) you serve, where they live/work, and how underserved they were/are.

- Describe their demographic and psychographic characteristics.

- Where are they physically? And are there boundaries of this work?

- How are they underserved and how do we know?

---

# Reason: an emotional and rational mix.

Some call it purpose, others call it *the why*. But it's not just words — it's the heartbeat of your brand. Strong fundraising doesn't simply state what you do; rather, it ignites action, sparks thought, and moves people. This is more than marketing speak. It's your north star.

This reason statement digs deeper than *the what* or *the how*. It's the very soul of your organization. When you communicate it right, you tap into trust, loyalty, and passion — the emotions that drive real connection with donors.

Your unshakable reason for being pulls your team through the most challenging nights and the longest days. It's the common thread that keeps everyone aligned and committed, no matter the storm.

## CLIENT EXAMPLES

*Justice Defenders: There can be no justice without peace, and there can be no peace without justice.*

*Peek Vision: Making the invisible, visible.*

*OceanMind: Because every citizen and future generation deserves the common heritage of humankind — healthy oceans and sustainable fisheries.*

---

As you can see, there are no formulas for coming up with the best reason. It can be a quotation, like the one above Justice Defenders pulled from Dr. Martin Luther King, Jr. Or it can be punchy and poetic with a double meaning, like the one Peek Vision used. Or just a statement, like OceanMind's. What's important is documenting your why, not exactly how it's written. And what's great about the examples above is that the nonprofit leaders we worked with here came up with them on their own. We just extracted the reasons from our conversations, so I know you can do this, too.

## ACTION STEP: ARTICULATE YOUR REASON

When your reason is clear, you often can't tell exactly what you do — because it's about your original motivation, not your current work.

- It's big and bold.

- It remains constant.

- It involves everyone.

- It has an "aha" effect.

- It's bigger than a goal.

- It comes from the heart.

With your reason down on paper, you should have now completed the need section of your theory of change. Well done.

But you also must communicate how you'll tackle said need, without complicating your mission (which complicates your fundraising). That's up next in Chapter 2: The Work.

# Summary.

1. The need section of your theory of change includes your problem, people, and reason.

2. Donors must understand the issue before they can care about your solution.

3. Your problem statement will be used throughout your marketing communications, from website header area to elevator pitch.

4. It's critical to name a specific group of people within the problem (note: those you serve here may be different from those you're trying to reach with your brand, which we'll name in the positioning strategy section).

5. Your reason (or purpose or why) gives your brand its emotional edge, yet is often missing from traditional logic models.

# 2. THE WORK

## Complicated missions complicate fundraising.

I once witnessed a tough conversation at a funder's annual conference. At the lunch table, two nonprofit co-founders had a chance to pitch a philanthropic foundation. But they stumbled through a mess of buzzwords — *empowerment*, *holistic*, *transformation*, *scalable*, *systems change*. It was a jargon salad.

The grantmaker, trying to make sense of it all, repeatedly asked, "What do you actually *do*?" But they couldn't get to the point. Eventually, she gave up, slid her business card across the table and gently said, "Why don't you visit our website. And if you think your work fits with what we fund, get in touch."

Brutal.

Too often, mission statements get tangled in unnecessary language. Then they lose meaning and end up forgotten. But here's the thing: your funders, your team, and those you serve don't want fluff. They want clarity.

That's why in this chapter, you'll learn how to clearly define your work: **inputs, interventions, partners, behaviors, big idea,** and **mission statement.** Your mission is most vital, so let's begin there and work our way backwards.

# Mission statement: mission critical.

"Not another lesson on mission statements," you moan.

Yes, because it's the most common donor grievance that we hear, by far: they don't understand what you actually do. And if a theory of change is the single most crucial tool in being fundable, then the mission is the most critical element in your theory of change.

It's worth repeating: many mission statements overuse buzzwords, especially jargon. Good mission statements are concise and useful — maybe even a bit dry.

> *"Doers: until proven otherwise, your first priority is to learn to clearly, concisely, and compellingly communicate what it is that you do." — Kevin Starr, institutional funder (United States)*

A succinct 8-word mission is a tool we borrow from Mulago Foundation.[1] As it gets to the heart of your work, by cutting out distractions.

"A good eight-word mission helps startups to evolve their big idea without getting pulled off track by their business model, the demands of funders, or the latest shiny object," Kevin Starr continues. "For more established organizations, it can be a guide through a necessary iterative process of re-design, helping them strip the hull of all the barnacles and unnecessary appendages that have accreted on the voyage so far."

## CLIENT EXAMPLES

*Humanity Crew: Preventing trauma with displaced children and their families.*

*JUST: Closing the racial wealth gap with Texas women.*

*STiR Education: Reigniting intrinsic motivation in teachers and education systems.*

---

As you can see in all three examples, there's a clear verb, a target population, and a desired outcome. And zero buzzwords.

---

## ACTION STEP: CRAFT YOUR 8-WORD MISSION

Our focus at this point is only to define the outcome you're trying to accomplish.

- It's expressed in eight words or fewer.

- It's formatted as a verb + target population + outcome.

- It doesn't use fluffy words like empowerment or transforming.

---

Now, you'll take the 8-word mission statement and build on it in order to develop your full mission statement below.

Layer on the type of organization you are. Words matter and people are literal. Are you a nonprofit? A charity? A social enterprise? Maybe a hybrid? An international NGO? A company?

Finally, bonus points if your mission statement clearly communicates what you do. This can be (but is not required to be) a summary of the interventions you will list soon.

---

**CLIENT EXAMPLES**

*Humanity Crew: A mental health aid organization that prevents trauma with displaced children and their families by providing emergency psychological interventions and training.*

*JUST: A nonprofit financial platform closing the racial wealth gap by investing in ambitious Texas women through capital, coaching, and community.*

*STiR Education: An international NGO that supports education systems to reignite intrinsic motivation in teachers and school officials via network meetings.*

---

These are the same three clients with their 8-word mission nestled within. Now, we've just added what they are and what they actually do. Simple, right?

**ACTION STEP: DEVELOP YOUR FULL MISSION STATEMENT**

Type of org + verb + a target population + an outcome, and details of your products, services, or programs.

- One sentence max!

- An average of 15–30 words.

- Avoid buzzwords; focus on what you do.

# Big idea: your distinctive idea of impact.

Defining your mission isn't enough for this work section of your theory of change. Because many organizations are tackling the same problem for the same people. Some might even have the same mission statement.

But very few (if any) should share your big idea.

Your big idea isn't about claiming that your team is better. Or touting some *external* value propositions (which we'll get to in the positioning section in Part Two). Rather, this big idea is *internal* — about your model. It's the core idea driving both your work and the impact you deliver. Focus on that.

## CLIENT EXAMPLES

*Cycle Connect: Loaning bikes as productive agriculture equipment.*

*Vega Coffee: Farmers roasting and shipping their own coffee.*

*Lively Minds: Rural parents as early childhood education providers.*

---

What's powerful about all three examples is that in a single phrase, they've defined how their model differs from all the other nonprofits in their space. As with Cycle Connect, other organizations also loan agriculture equipment, but who else starts with a bike? Of all the coffee social enterprises around the globe, have you ever heard of a nonprofit (other than Vega Coffee) that trains farmers to roast and ship their own coffee right from the source? And finally, while countless education interventions exist in Africa, who else but Lively Minds is using rural parents to deliver the curriculum? These three big ideas need no further explanation.

## ACTION STEP: DETERMINE YOUR BIG IDEA

Boil your idea down to a few words that capture your special sauce. This distillation of your idea to its essence will both help you communicate it and improve it.

- What makes your model special compared to others?

- Why does your work create more impact than other organizations?

- What's your distinctive spin on solving this problem for these people?

All that said, be aware that "Not everything needs to be novel or innovative, just that the specific combo of what you are doing, for/with whom you are doing it, and where you are doing it is not currently being done," advises political and behavioral scientist, Heather Elisabeth Lanthorn.

"And that if you disappeared, a real gap would be left."

# Behaviors: motivators – barriers = change.

Focus on your mission and your big idea all you want, but impact doesn't happen by itself.

For your mission to succeed, the people you mentioned in the need section have to shift their behaviors, too. So this element helps funders see that you've mapped out the full journey.

In short: impact comes from the intersection of your own interventions, the work of your partner organizations, plus the behaviors of the people you serve.

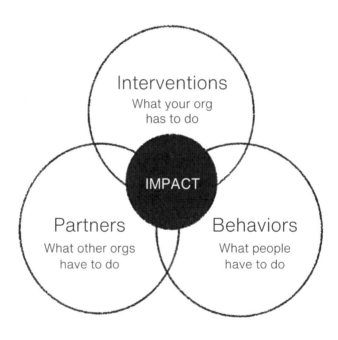

FIGURE 4: The intersection of impact.

**CLIENT EXAMPLE: WAVES FOR WATER**

- *Families properly use filtration systems to purify unsafe water before drinking.*

- *Communities adequately clean and maintain rainwater harvesting systems and filters.*

---

The truth is, Waves for Water could do its work perfectly (which is to build filtration and rainwater harvesting systems). They could raise a ton of money for it and find great partners. But if their families and communities (the people they serve) aren't involved in the long run, the theory of change falls apart.

---

**ACTION STEP: DECIDE WHICH BEHAVIORS NEED TO CHANGE**

Think back to the people in the need section. What behavior must they change for you to best drive impact?

- A single sentence that includes the people and the behavior.

- Not answering how, but rather what needs to change.

- Attitudes and feelings don't count here — only actions do.

# Partners: areas outside your interventions.

Now let's get clear on what you're *not* going to do. Setting your focus is crucial here. Donors aren't looking for a jack-of-all-trades; most of them want a master of one mission. They need to see you're zeroing in on what truly matters.

Admit you can't do everything. And it's smart to acknowledge where others are stronger. Funders increasingly value partnerships, so show them you're all about teamwork.

**CLIENT EXAMPLES**

*PEAS partners: Feeder primary schools; livelihoods/TVET institutions; universities and teacher training colleges; influential advocacy organizations.*

*Justice Defenders partners: Improving prison conditions; providing legal services for the poor; striving for advocacy or policy change; working with the judiciary; supporting rehab or reintegration.*

With PEAS, it was important to show that — while they were focused on secondary education — other players were critical in their model. They listed types of organizations they could partner with. Whereas with Justice Defenders, they previously did most of this work themselves. But when we focused their theory of change around justice alone, they knew these categories would become partner interventions — no longer their own. So instead of types of organizations, they listed types of interventions. Either way is fine.

## ACTION STEP: SAY WHAT PARTNERS WILL DO

List key partners you already work with to achieve your mission. Then, list partners you wish you could work with to better your work and serve your people.

- Who are the partners (categories, not actual organization names)?

- What do they do?

- What needs to change for you to collaborate with them?

# Interventions: laser focus.

If you've used a logic model before, you might know this part as activities instead of interventions. These are the core programs or products you focus on.

Many organizations do juggle a lot, but this is about homing in on the main pillars of your work.

Remember, changing behavior is far from simple. If your model has more than three to five key interventions, it will be tough to execute, communicate, and fundraise around.

So stick to what you can nail.

## CLIENT EXAMPLES

Note that these are the same two clients from the partners section, so that you could see what they DON'T do first, and now what they DO do.

*PEAS: Build and run PEAS schools; partner with other schools to implement practices; research evidence to influence policy and practice; co-design programs with governments.*

*Justice Defenders: Education (facilitating law students); Training (creating curriculum, training paralegals, running the secondment program); Practice (legal practice, file tracing, advocating on cases, collaborating with pro bono partners).*

---

With both clients, we wanted only three to four things that each client could easily tell donors about. Bonus points if you can bucket them like Justice Defenders into three single words (Education, Training, and Practice). These single words work well (instead of a long sentence) in places like your website, e.g., under What We Do in the drop-down menu.

**ACTION STEP: LIST YOUR INTERVENTIONS**

First consider what partners are already doing or could do. Then write down — in brief — the categories of work you have to control.

- Think of three or four specific interventions and activities.

- List the things you must execute (the activities you're uniquely qualified to own).

# Inputs: resources for the journey.

And finally, before you start your impact journey you need to know what it will take to reach the summit.

Think of it like prepping for that big hike up the mountain we talked about earlier. You wouldn't hit the trails without packing your bags first and taking some water. The climb ahead requires the right inputs.

Your resources could be physical, like goods or cash, or something less tangible, like time or brand strength. But let's not kid ourselves — money usually tops the list.

So state it plainly. Make it clear what you need to move forward with your mission.

## CLIENT EXAMPLE: GREEN FORUM SWEDEN

- *Unrestricted funding*

- *Secretariat staff*

- *Tech systems*

- *Local green partners*

- *Strong brand communications*

---

As you can see, these resources aren't super strategic. But listing them all in your theory of change gives donors and partners options for how to engage with you. And it ensures you and your team are crystal clear on what's needed before telling the world about your grand vision ahead.

## ACTION STEP: DECIDE WHICH INPUTS ARE REQUIRED

Think about the interventions and mission you just listed. Then write down all the resources needed. Even if they're not realistic at this point, be honest about what is required to pull off your ambition.

- Don't worry about specific figures (e.g., amount of money needed).

- It's better to list more than is needed. You can always pare back.

In the last two chapters, you've defined *why* you exist and *what* you do. Up next is the final section of your theory of change: *where* you're going (the desired results).

So in Chapter 3, you'll learn how to sell donors on your vision, not just your cause.

# Summary.

1. The work section of your theory of change contains your inputs, interventions, partners, behaviors, big idea, and mission statement.

2. The most common complaint we hear from funders: they don't understand what you do. So a mission statement is the most crucial sentence in your fundraising communications.

3. Since many organizations might have the same mission or interventions, your big idea showcases the secret sauce of how you create more and better impact.

4. Your community also has agency in creating change for themselves and others, so name their behaviors in your theory of change.

5. It's vital to list the closely-related and important interventions that partners will handle (these are things that you *don't do*).

6. Most nonprofits can't pull off more than three to five interventions at once. So focus.

# 3. THE RESULTS

## Sell donors on your vision, not just your cause.

Stop for a minute and think about the most outstanding world leaders throughout time. Those who inspired humanity, mobilized forces effectively, and changed the course of history for the better.

Martin Luther King Jr. had a dream of unity. Gandhi inspired a nation toward independence. Yaa Asantewaa led an Asante army against British colonizers. And Ruth Bader Ginsburg pioneered for equality. These social justice leaders didn't just take action; they had a vision — a clear, powerful vision that drove change.

That's why your job is to speak vision into existence. To persuade like-minded funders and staff to join your audacious movement. And to map the stars, not just the steps. Because most great social justice activists are like storytellers from the future, fearlessly telling us what is coming. Not merely focusing on the impact itself.

So for people to follow you — and funders to fund your mission — they must understand where you're going.

In this chapter you'll learn how to define the results. Including your **pathway, outputs, outcomes, 10-year target,**[1] and **vision statement.** But since vision is the main element of this part, we'll start there and work back through the rest.

*"Visionaries will always meet opposition from weak minds, but the seeds they plant always save the world."* — Bangambiki Habyarimana, community worker (Rwanda)

## Vision statement: an envisioned endgame.

A vision statement is one part strategy, one part narrative. It takes both your imagination and desired future state. Then it weaves them through effective copywriting to communicate your plans succinctly and powerfully.

The power of vision has been proven in business literature. James Collins and Jerry Porras studied hundreds of organizations in the book *Built to Last: Successful Habits of Visionary Companies*.[2] Their research demonstrated that since the year 1925, companies with a clear vision have outperformed their competitors by a factor of 12.

A good vision is tangible, energizing, and highly focused. People get it right away; it takes little or no explanation. A vision statement clearly describes the ultimate change you want to see. And a vision can be crafted through various lenses, for example:

"A world without..."

"A planet with..."

"A company that reaches..."

"A nature conservation sector that thrives on..."

**CLIENT EXAMPLES**

*Muso Health: Universal health care — for all people, without delay.*

*Basmeh & Zeitooneh* بسمة وزيتونة: *A constructive society that lives with dignity.*

*BloodWater: To share in the joy and wonder of seeing the end of HIV/AIDS and water crises in our lifetime.*

---

As you can tell, there's not one perfect way to write a vision statement.

---

**ACTION STEP: CAST YOUR VISION**

What does the end state you want to help create look like? What will lives look like when you successfully deliver on your vision?

- One sentence max!

- Average of 15–30 words.

- Make it both tangible and inspirational.

- It's often the walk-off-stage moment — the end state you're striving for.

---

Unfortunately, a *Forbes* study found that 70% of employees don't grasp their company's vision. And if you don't have a clear vision, your fundraising will falter. The most common vision statement mistakes we see are not putting it on paper, mixing mission and vision, changing your vision too often, using cliche language, and not making it an end-state.

> *"Visionary leadership and good vision statements are prophetic. Articulating a vision clearly brings it into being and generates the funding to enable that future reality."*
> — Michelle L Christian, governance advisor (Canada)

# 10-year target: setting sights on the horizon.

Most enduring leaders and thriving organizations have something in common: they set massive, long-term targets. Sometimes called a big, hairy, audacious goal (BHAG), 10 years is about the right amount of time for this target. But this isn't merely a goal; it's a magnet. It draws in supporters, energizes your team, and directs your short-term plans.

True success comes when your vision (covered previously) is so big that no one can achieve it alone. But your organization *should* be able to reach this 10-year target on its own.

Have you ever noticed all the nonprofits successfully fundraising with messaging like, "By 2030 this, millions of this and that..." plastered all over their communications? Funders love this type of audacious thinking.

**CLIENT EXAMPLES**

*Peek Vision: By 2050, reverse the global curve and prevent 1.25 billion people from untreated vision loss.*

*Reach for Change: We'll support 3,000 social entrepreneurs to change the lives of 30 million children and youth by 2030.*

*Community Health Impact Coalition: 95+ low- and middle-income countries adopt professional community health worker (CHW) policies.*

---

These three examples share two qualities. There's a big hairy number, and in theory these targets could be accomplished.

---

**ACTION STEP: SET YOUR 10-YEAR TARGET**

What is the target? What's the date?

- You'll know the right target when you have it.

- It's measurable, achievable, and time-bound.

- It can be target-oriented, competitive, based on a role model, or focused on internal transformation.

# Outcomes: changes in conditions.

Master the difference between outcomes and outputs, and watch your funding grow. Why? Because outcomes show real change, not simply effort. Outputs are what you do; outcomes are the impact of what you do.

It's the difference between saying you planted seeds and showing that you grew a forest.

There are long- and short-term outcomes. Long-term outcomes typically take 24+ months to see and/or measure. But every model is different. Outcomes in areas like education, for example, can take years.

Short-term outcomes usually show up between 6–12 months after the work is done. But it could be weeks, depending on your interventions.

Bonus points if you can identify a singular short-term outcome. By obsessively focusing on a near-term change in conditions, you can unlock long-term changes in several ways.

## CLIENT EXAMPLE: HUMANITY CREW

- *Short-term: Reduced trauma and stress-related disorders in displaced children.*

- *Long-term: Increased ability of children and their families to integrate into host communities or resettle back home; decreased financial and social burden caused by mental health disorders; decreased premature mortality from non-communicable diseases through mental health prevention.*

How powerful a story to tell donors: that everything they do in the short-term is focused on this single outcome. And that this single outcome can cause a ripple effect of countless more outcomes over the long run. That's being fundable.

## ACTION STEP: DETERMINE YOUR DESIRED OUTCOMES

If you've done your best work, what positive changes in conditions do your people feel after six, 12, or 24 months? And what changes in conditions are required to reach your vision?

- Outcomes typically can't be counted with simple math.

- Outcomes aren't about you — they're about those you serve.

- Outcomes often can't be measured if you're just sitting in your office.

# Outputs: leading indicators to track.

Outputs are about what you've produced. They're useful for tracking what you did and where you spent money, but they're just a starting point, not the finish line. Outputs show effort toward impact (or outcomes), not impact itself.

Despite the classic logic model that has existed for decades (which includes a column for outcomes), many organizations stop after measuring these outputs alone. And most savvy funders now demand evidence around both outcomes and impact. They want to see actual changes in conditions on the ground.

Outcomes trump outputs — always.

**CLIENT EXAMPLE: JUST**

- *Number of clients and Just Entrepreneur Trust Agents*
- *Weekly group meeting attendance rate*
- *Amount of capital received by clients*
- *Online community participation*
- *Retention rate to second loan*
- *Percentage on-time payment*
- *Number of goals set*

Can you tell if they've created any impact from these measures? No. And while, yes, this nonprofit does create significant impact, a funder wouldn't know it from the list above. Sadly, many organizations stop short and only share this type of outputs list.

**ACTION STEP: LIST YOUR EXPECTED OUTPUTS**

Think about the measures needed to drive your desired outcomes. Don't worry about exact numbers, but rather what needs to be produced or counted.

- Outputs are usually described with numbers.

- Outputs should be relatively easy to count or observe.

- Outputs let you know within days or weeks if your programs are on track.

# Pick your pathway: scale back the buzzwords.

The social sector has abused the word *scale*.

Worn out the term *systems change*.

Then nonprofit leaders feel pressured by funders to contort into something they're not. (Not to mention that those who *are* scaling and *are* changing systems get lost in the twisted jargon.)

So, here's a challenge for you nonprofit leaders as you raise money.

Scale and systems change are not the only paths ahead for you. There are actually four impact pathways — thus, four messaging options for your fundraising and brand, as shown in Figure 5.

Unsurprisingly, organizations can only pursue one or two of these pathways well. But once you decide on your pathway(s), you can build your desired organization and communicate about it confidently. You can also match most foundations to these pathways. So don't seek grants from a scale-focused funder when, in reality, sustainability is your best path.

Let's explore these four pathways further, using our former education clients as examples.

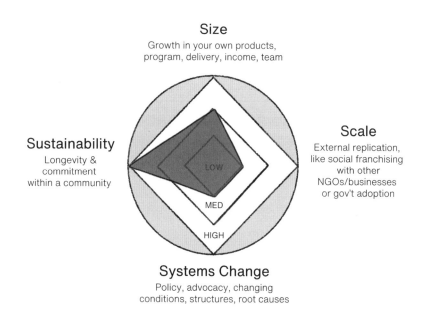

FIGURE 5: The Mighty Ally pathways tool.

## Size.

The size pathway means that you grow in your products, programs, delivery, income, and team. As in, your organization itself gets bigger. This pathway seems straightforward, but back to what I said in the introduction: only one in 1,000 nonprofits grows beyond a small business.

### CLIENT EXAMPLE: EDUCATION DEVELOPMENT TRUST

*Revenue and international team growth via major education reform projects.*

## Scale.

The scale pathway demands external replication, like social franchising or government adoption. As in, your innovation or program takes off without you always being involved. This pathway differs from *scaling up* your organization (see the size pathway). Scale means quite the opposite.

### CLIENT EXAMPLE: STIR EDUCATION

*National government adoption with controlled demonstration districts.*

## Sustainability.

The sustainability pathway implies longevity and commitment within a community (an inch wide, a mile deep). As in, simply stick around and serve a specific group of people for the long haul. We need more organizations to be OK with embracing this noble pathway — as there is plenty of hard work to do and many donors to fund it.

**CLIENT EXAMPLE: NYAKA**

*25 years of child-centered education in the same rural communities.*

## Systems change.

The systems change pathway involves policy, advocacy, changing conditions, structures, and root causes. As in, you end the suffering in the first place. The best description I've ever heard for systems change is actually an unrelated quote from Desmond Tutu, the beloved late bishop in South Africa. He said, "There comes a point where we need to stop just pulling people out of the river. We need to go upstream and find out why they're falling in."

Another gem of wisdom is from nonprofit leader Perry Boyle, who gives an acid test for systems change: "If you stop your intervention, what happens? If you can't stop intervening to get impact, the system hasn't changed."

That's one reason why working *with* or *within* systems differs significantly from *changing* them.

## CLIENT EXAMPLE: COALITION FOR GOOD SCHOOLS

*Practitioners and policymakers, preventing violence against children in schools.*

To be clear: scale and systems change are fundamental to advancing social justice. Just not for many (most?) nonprofits that are too small or simply not built for those more-nuanced pathways.

And these four pathways have no shared definition. That's part of the problem.

But with this pathways tool — along with all the other elements we've just covered in Chapter 3 — you can build an authentic and effective brand. Not one that's only trying to appeal to donors.

## ACTION STEP: PICK YOUR PATHWAY

If you had to pick one of the options below, which pathway gives you the best chance of achieving your vision?

- **Size:** Growth in your own products, programs, delivery, income, team.

- **Sustainability:** Longevity and commitment within a community.

- **Scale:** External replication, like social franchising or government adoption.

- **Systems change:** Policy, advocacy, changing conditions, structures, root causes.

This pathways tool is an action step that will certainly take some leadership conversation and a great deal of time thinking about it. No stress, though, since most nonprofits haven't thought about this one before, either!

Congratulations. You've made it through the entire theory of change section. With your theory of change complete, you're now halfway to being fundable.

The other half? Devising a strategic plan — the topic of the next section.

Before we go, let's connect and condense your theory of change in this popular action step.

---

**ACTION STEP: CLARIFY YOUR ENTIRE MODEL WITH A ONE-SENTENCE THEORY OF CHANGE**

This tool is just six pieces and one sentence. But it can summarize your entire theory of change in a single one-liner. The formula below consists of your problem + people + mission + interventions + 10-year target.

> **Because (WHY), we work (WHERE) to help (WHO) (WHAT) (HOW), in order to (WHEN).**

---

## CLIENT EXAMPLES

*Sabre Education: Because 90% of a child's brain develops before age five (WHY), we work in Ghana (WHERE) to help the early childhood education sector (WHO) provide the best possible early childhood education (WHAT) by partnering with government to implement play-based learning at scale (HOW), in order to achieve Sustainable Development Goal 4.2 by 2030 (WHEN).*

*Transform Schools: Because poverty could be cut in half if all children completed secondary school (WHY), we work in India (WHERE) to help secondary school system actors (WHO) improve learning outcomes for children (WHAT) through co-designed learning enhancement programs and capacity building (HOW), in order to reach 20 million children by 2030 (WHEN).*

---

True, both of these are long, clunky sentences. But they're not supposed to be a formal elevator pitch or official copywriting. Instead, coming up with an effective one-liner is meant to drive brand focus and achieve strategic clarity.

# Summary.

1.  The results section of your theory of change includes your pathway, outputs, short- and long-term outcomes, 10-year target, and vision.

2.  Vision statements are critical for fundraising, but most are either flawed, or stuck in a leader's head, or altogether missing from a theory of change.

3.  Since vision statements are often lifetimes away, aiming at a 10-year target is valuable for funding and linking your theory of change to your strategic plan.

4.  Outputs and outcomes might sound similar, but couldn't be more different in what story they tell to donors about impact (or not).

5.  Scale and systems change might make the most noise in the social sector, but there are four viable pathways to impact — pick one or two.

# STRATEGIC PLAN
Turn your theory into traction and provide proof to funders with this communications tool.

We had an early nonprofit client whose massive strategic plan consisted of eight elements to their 2030 vision. The plan had five goals within each of the eight 2030 visions. And six sub-goals within each goal. It had another five key areas plus a separate set of vague objectives — none of which laddered up or down to the visions, goals, or sub-goals.

Confused? We were too.

What's telling is that in the year Mighty Ally worked with them, not a single team member mentioned their plan. Or showed it in their fundraising conversations. Much less used it to make decisions.

We've all seen this type of strategic plan. It's neither actionable nor measurable. It's all strategy, no plan. All vision, no tactics — leaving nonprofit brands with big dreams but no mechanisms to realize their potential. No wonder funders don't buy it. And no wonder 67% of strategic plans fail, according to *Inc. Magazine*.

Anyone can set a strategy. But a lot fewer can map out the plan to execute it. So in this section, you'll learn more about a strategic plan: **what it is, why it matters,** and **how to create one.** Then you'll fully work on the three main parts of your strategic plan in Chapters 4, 5, and 6.

> *"Action without thought is empty. Thought without action is blind."* — *Kwame Nkrumah, politician (Ghana)*

## What it is.

At Mighty Ally, we use a brand-centric definition of strategic planning. In the previous section, we covered that your theory of change is about showing donors:

**Why** you exist.

**What** you do.

**Where** you're going.

So in this section, your strategic plan shows donors the other bookend:

**Who** will get it done.

**When** it will be done.

**How** you'll get it done.

That's it.

A strategic plan is a communications tool — for both your team and your donors. You can't clean polluted water with a strategic plan. It doesn't cure illness. Nor does it educate a child. It's simply words on a page. Otherwise known as: communications.

Yet, too many nonprofit leaders see a strategic plan as a huge document they're forced to produce every few years to appease their donors. Or think strategic planning is a series of painful, offsite meetings with distant consultants to appease their boards.

Then it's done and dusted. Long forgotten. Never communicated, neither to our teams nor back to future donors.

That's why we're not just talking about your strategic *plan* — the thing, the document, the noun. We're also talking about strategic *planning* — the action, the processes, the verb.

> *"Strategy is not something that happens at a point in time — it happens constantly. It's always in motion… and should be driving more than just a bunch of meetings among a select few that result in some PowerPoint slides that could land with a thud." — Delve*[1]

Your strategic plan is also valuable immediately. Not just in the long term. Because it's half of becoming fundable. Even for small nonprofits in firefighting mode — trying to raise enough money to stay alive — your strategy should help you right away in fundraising.

# Why it matters: maximized funding.

Defining the work within your theory of change gets you started, but you also have to show donors that you're doing said work. In other words, your ambition must become action.

A major family foundation once told me:

The number one reason they don't invest is not the idea itself. It's when they don't believe the organization can execute its idea. So why, they wonder, communicate a grand vision (in your theory of change) without taking calculated steps to achieve it (in this strategic plan)? Your strategic plan proves to funders that you can back up your ambition.

Any individual in the organization should know what they must do — today! — to best achieve the vision ahead. And it's powerful for funders to see everyone on a team rowing in the same direction.

*"We have a strategic plan. It's called doing things."*
*— Herb Kelleher, airline CEO (United States)*

# How to create your strategic plan.

We've spent years using (and abusing!) various strategic planning formats. From Gazelles' One Page Strategic Plan to Paterson StratOp, to McKinsey's 7S Framework to the Entrepreneurial Operating System (EOS®). But no standard exists for nonprofits. So Mighty Ally took inspiration from these private sector sources and created a new model for nonprofits.

(By the way, the best planning model I have ever used in the private sector was EOS. It comes from the best-selling book, *Traction: Get a Grip on Your Business* by Gino Wickman.[2] EOS itself is built upon the ideas and tools of many books before it. So if you like the brief taste of what's below and want to dig much more deeply into running your organization — go buy *Traction*.)

For now, here's the high-level summary of our strategic plan process:

**Team:** In Chapter 4 you will focus on turning everybody into a fundraiser, establishing your core values, then getting the right people in the right seats and the wrong people off the bus.

**Priorities:** In Chapter 5 you'll break down the 10-year target from your theory of change into a three-year picture, annual goals, and quarterly projects.

**Rhythms:** Then in Chapter 6 you can set a pattern for how to get the work done via impact processes, internal communications, and tracking key performance indicators (KPIs).

You should be able to capture the highlights of your entire strategic plan in a single-page blueprint. Like the one in Figure 6. Similar to the theory of change blueprint in the previous section, this blueprint becomes a powerful tool to flash on screen during a donor conversation.

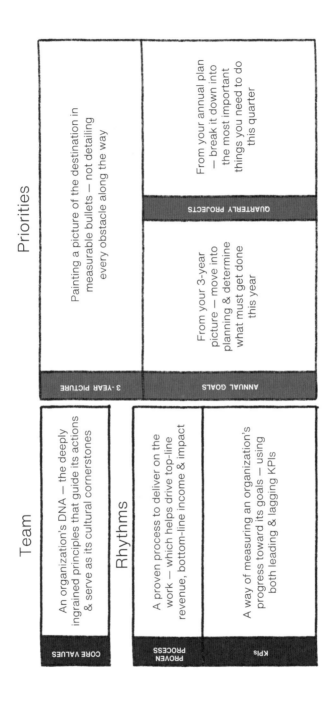

## Priorities

**3-YEAR PICTURE**
Painting a picture of the destination in measurable bullets — not detailing every obstacle along the way

**ANNUAL GOALS**
From your 3-year picture — move into planning & determine what must get done this year

**QUARTERLY PROJECTS**
From your annual plan — break it down into the most important things you need to do this quarter

## Team

**CORE VALUES**
An organization's DNA — the deeply ingrained principles that guide its actions & serve as its cultural cornerstones

## Rhythms

**PROVEN PROCESS**
A proven process to deliver on the work — which helps drive top-line revenue, bottom-line income & impact

**KPIs**
A way of measuring an organization's progress toward its goals — using both leading & lagging KPIs

FIGURE 6: The Mighty Ally strategic plan blueprint.
(Download an editable copy of this tool and other templates in this book via our self-paced, online course at mightyally.org/course.)

As you can see, strategic planning isn't rocket science. Thought-provoking and demanding, sure. But hard to understand? No.

If you're this far into the book and thinking this all feels too overwhelming to tackle right now — it's not. I'm not asking you to follow a process we don't use ourselves. And we're not talking about the typical, massive, high-production strategic plans that often take months to decide and design. Those are outdated by the time they ship.

Instead, treat your strategic plan as a living, breathing tool where function trumps form. It's pointed to in meetings, printed out on office walls, and updated multiple times a year. So it doesn't need to be pretty or wordy — it's meant to drive alignment and action. Not win design or writing awards. So whether you have 15 minutes or 15 hours to spend on this section, just start now and write down what you know to be true today.

## A strategy's strength isn't its length.

And finally, a quick story to illustrate the point before we wrap this section.

In 1990, when Sega created the Sonic the Hedgehog game to compete with Nintendo's dominant Mario franchise, a classic David vs. Goliath story emerged.

(Perhaps like some of you grassroots nonprofit leaders trying to fundraise alongside international NGOs.)

How did Sega communicate its new strategy? Not with exhaustive spreadsheets. Not endless presentations. Not 50-page documents. It was the simple plan below, with five goals and 14 words total.[3]

## The Battle Plan

### 1. Lower the price

### 2. Defeat Mario

### 3. More sports

### 4. Cool for teens

### 5. Make fun of Nintendo

Beautiful strategic thinking, turned into beautiful messaging. And they won. Within two years, Sega captured 65% market share.

The takeaway for your brand?

It's not only *which* strategy you're communicating. It's also *how* you're communicating it. The strategic plan itself is only half the battle; the other half involves the mastery of delivering it. Because your big ideas — however brilliant — are worthless if lost in translation or easily forgotten by donors or even your own team.

Confidence speaks briefly; fear speaks at length. Your team craves clarity. Your funders crave clarity. Your community craves clarity.

So make your next strategy the briefest (and boldest) yet. Aim for a plan that's short and shrewd. Condense to convince.

We use a Google Slides template because it forces brevity. This will be a document you update constantly, so the process must be agile. Your team must be agile, too. That's exactly what we'll start to unpack together in Chapter 4, coming up next.

*"Ambition never comes to an end."* — *Kenneth Kaunda, former president (Zambia)*

# Summary.

1. A good strategic plan consists of the following three parts: team, priorities, and rhythms.

2. Most strategic plans fail. And the main reason is that they're all thinking, no tactics.

3. A strategic plan is a communications tool, because it consists of words on a page meant to convey how you will act on your ambition.

4. This plan is a critical piece of your fundraising toolkit, because it gives funders proof that you can pull off your claims (or have already done so!).

5. Your strategic plan should be linked to your theory of change — in particular, the 10-year target from your theory of change is broken down into your strategic plan's three-year picture.

# 4. TEAM

## Fundraising starts with boards and teams, not tactics.

Look at the brightest nonprofit brands that raise the most money in our social sector. Then glance at their team page. You'll find — almost without fail — a dedicated brand communications staff. Plus, heavy fundraising ownership from the CEO.

Brand management is not a part-time function of a part-time fundraising director. It's not meant to be a side job for the operations coordinator who took a Photoshop class at university. And it's definitely not a cousin's freelancer friend doing some pro-bono marketing. Similarly, fundraising can never be a part-time function of a part-time programs director.

When these roles are an afterthought, a game-changing brand plan or fundraising strategy will die on the vine without anyone to grow it.

That's why:

**Good:** brand tactics.

**Better:** brand strategy.

**Best:** brand team.

There's an old adage, "first who, then what." That's why your strategic plan team section is so critical for brand building.

In this chapter you'll learn **why communications officers aren't fundraising unicorns,** then how to **turn every voice into a funding force, establish your core values,** and **get the right people in the right seats.**

Brilliance begins with your team. Hire, then inspire.

# Fundraising, communications, digital marketing, graphic design, PR, writing, photo/video, website development, and event planning... are not all one job.[1]

As you think about team roles for fundraising, remember: your solo Communications Manager is not a unicorn. They are not a miracle maker.

Yes, they're outstanding. Yes, a Jill-of-all-trades. Yes, a task tamer, too. But no, it's not fair to think that a one-person comms team can pull off countless jobs perfectly. (Not without burning out.)

Even worse is the unrealistic expectations of a single Manager of Fundraising and Communications — with zero staff. That's trying to milk two different departments out of one brave soul.

So, nonprofit leaders, you have two options:

**Adjust your expectations:** If you can only hire a generalist Communications Manager (often just out of university!), accept that none of your comms channels will be world-class. No shame, because that's probably all you can afford. Just stop comparing your brand to big charities with big professionals handling big professions. Your Comms Manager is doing an incredible job already, keeping all the balls in the air.

**Invest in specialists:** If you don't want your brand to be second best at everything, put your money where your mouth is. Hire a copywriting expert. Hire a graphic design pro. Hire a social media wiz. And so on. Then your Comms Manager can play the orchestra conductor role, bringing all these specialists together well in harmonious play. Funding will follow, but you must invest in brand first.

Don't just take my word for it.

> *"How big should your comms team be? That's a very different question from how big your team probably is. We often see one-person communications teams in very large organizations that should frankly know better and be investing a whole lot more."* — *Kivi Leroux Miller, nonprofit marketing author (United States)*

The annual Nonprofit Communications Trends Report shows that communications team effectiveness increases dramatically once you hit three full-time people. And the average comms team sizes per nonprofit budget are the following:

- **Up to $500,000:** 1.4 full-time staff.

- **$500,000 to $1M:** 1.8 full-time staff.

- **$1M to $5M:** 2 full-time staff.

- **$5.1M to $20M:** 2.9 full-time staff.

- **$20M plus:** 4.2 full-time staff.

So the choice is yours. Just remember that the overburdened Comms Manager is a systemic nonprofit issue. They're some of the most talented and tireless — but tired — people we meet.

Expecting one person to juggle it all? Expecting a magical brand? Time for a reality check.

## What you *think* your comms department needs...

## What it actually needs...

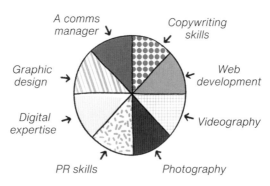

FIGURE 7: Your solo Communications Manager is not a unicorn.

# Every voice: a funding force.

We always hear the question from nonprofit leaders: how do I get my team and board to care more about fundraising? And we always hear from teams and boards: why am I being asked to fundraise?

> *"Nonprofits often experience a schism between those on the program side and those raising money to pay the bills, with fundraising often viewed as a kind of grunt work that happens separately from core advocacy or services. This can lead to resentment and burnout among development professionals, but also weaker fundraising."*
> *— Dawn Wolfe, philanthropy author (United States)*

The majority of fundraising is good *communications*. That's why every team (and board!) member is a potential touchpoint for your brand. Dare I say, a potential fundraiser too? Because every one of their emails, meetings, networking events, field visits, social posts, or conferences is like a mini donor campaign.

> *"Not everyone on your team is going to be confident or comfortable with asking, but that doesn't mean they don't play important roles in fundraising." — Darian Rodriguez Heyman, fundraising author (United States)*

So here's how to make your entire team — plus your board — responsible for fundraising. It's a mental model from the book *The*

*AAA Way to Fundraising Success*, by Kay Sprinkel Grace.[2] Just assign each person one of three roles in donor communications:

- **The Ambassador**
- **The Advocate**
- **The Asker**

## Everyone is an Ambassador.

Ambassadors open doors and build rapport, which is essential for any board or team member. They're the face of the organization, trained to carry your message with a non-negotiable zeal.

Ambassadors lay the groundwork for potential donor engagement. They make warm hand-offs for further action. So, if they're not passionate, they shouldn't be on your team. Enthusiasm is a prerequisite. And no one is excused.

## Advocates speak up and out.

Advocates deepen engagement by articulating your cause, like educating others or speaking at events. They solidify credibility, present your mission using deep knowledge, and address challenging questions.

Advocates are pivotal in turning casual interest led by Ambassadors into committed support. Here's the difference: Ambassadors make friends. Advocates make the case.

## Askers close with confidence.

Askers are the closers in your fundraising strategy, adept at converting interest into action. Effective Askers are also good listeners — able to tailor their approach based on donor feedback.

Askers embody the spirit of both Ambassadors and Advocates, but with a focused aim: to secure funding. Askers must be well-trained and confident to handle the responsibilities of soliciting donations.

---

### ACTION STEP: DETERMINE YOUR ADVOCATES AND ASKERS

Since everyone on the team is an Ambassador by default, ensure that they're all trained to use your basic messaging (coming up in Chapter 11). Then decide who will be an Advocate. Who will speak at public events? Who will host webinars, etc.? These Advocates need deeper messaging on "making the case" for why you're different, the impact you create, and more. Finally, a select few team members will be Askers. Those should be obvious, as they're typically the founder(s), plus members of the leadership team and other fundraising staff.

---

## Core values: people who fit.

To turn every voice into a funding force, first ensure each person reflects your values. Your organization's values are its DNA — the core principles that shape every action and decision. These are the cornerstones that keep donors coming back, year after year.

These values must never be compromised for convenience or to get a quick buck from funders. The values must be embedded in every aspect of your brand, from internal operations to public messaging.

*"While a brand can be defined as the outward manifestation of a company's DNA, culture is where your brand is born."*
— Tony Hsieh, business leader (United States)

Clear values attract like-minded individuals — and like-minded donors too — who align with your brand, while naturally weeding out those who don't. Once set, these values should guide every decision: hiring, firing, reviewing, and rewarding. This is how you build a strong fundraising culture.

### CLIENT EXAMPLE: STIR EDUCATION

- *Humility: We don't have all of the answers upfront.*

- *Ownership: We trust each other with high expectations.*

- *Openness: We will listen, learn, and improve.*

- *Purpose: We're united by a shared vision we'll achieve together.*

This is an excellent set of core values for three reasons. First, they're not all the same cliche values that other organizations pick. Second, they have a single main word, plus a quick sentence to describe each word, to ensure everyone knows what they mean. And finally, they spell HOOP which speaks to STiR's model and makes the values easy to remember. In fact, a unique set of values like HOOP can become a great donor selling point.

## ACTION STEP: DECIDE YOUR CORE VALUES

List the qualities of your best people who, if combined into one and cloned, could lead you to accomplish your vision.

- Single words or simple statements.

- 3–5 per person in mind, then combine into five or so for the organization.

- Could these be valid in 100 years? Would you hold those values even if one or more of them became a competitive disadvantage?

# Right people in the right seats.

So you established your core values: check. How do you use them?

Jim Collins nails it in his book *Good to Great*: get the right people on the bus, in the right seats, and get the wrong ones off. Then, and only then, decide where to drive.

The right people are those who share your core values and thrive in your culture. The right seat, however, means they're working in the area where they're most skilled and passionate. You might have the right person in the wrong seat. They're likely valuable and worth moving to a better role. But if someone is in the right seat but isn't the right fit for the organization, they need to go.

While leaders are often seen as the face of an organization, your employees have a much broader reach and can greatly influence fundraising. They're on the front lines — answering calls, visiting participants, meeting funders. This collective power can shape your brand more than any marketing effort. So invest wisely in this area, both in time and in resources. And don't forget: your board is part of this team equation, too.

As you evaluate your people, you might see a glaring gap: right at the top. If you're a solo founder, you fight a sobering (but silent) reality: 80% of all billion-dollar unicorn companies had two or more co-founders.[3]

It's hard enough to grow your fundraising. It's even more challenging in the social sector, where one in three charities fail within just 10 years.[4] And where half of nonprofit CEOs become the top executive in their 20s — some even in their teens![5]

But it's most difficult without another founder or two.

So, consider true co-founders. Sure, a strong leadership team can help. But those leaders come and go. It's not the same as having your name on the papers, reputation on the line, or skin in the game. Even if it has been years since the original founding, you can still bring on another founder or owner.

And don't forget to push the board/donors for help. Boards (and donors) aren't just there for accountability and money. They should provide you with their work and wisdom as well. So if you must chase and guide your board — instead of vice versa — there's an imbalance.

Make no mistake: all you solo nonprofit founders deserve a massive shout-out. As well as acknowledgment from boards and donors that what you're doing is tremendous, tenacious, and rare.

You are seen.

You deserve support.

We're all in this together.

So what do you do with your team once you have the right people in the right seats? You set your priorities. Because anything is possible, but everything isn't.

That's the topic of Chapter 5, up next.

# Summary.

1. The team section of your strategic plan includes core values, the right people, and the right seats.

2. The adage "first who, then what" reminds us that the best plans will come to nothing without the right team.

3. The overburdened comms/fundraising/design officer is one role to fix.

4. Core values are how we ensure that we attract then retain the right people for our brand.

5. Not everyone on your team is a fundraising Asker, but any team or board member is a fundraiser by virtue of being an Ambassador or an Advocate.

# 5. PRIORITIES
Anything is possible. Everything isn't.

Kongō Gumi was a Buddhist temple construction company founded in 578 AD. It remained the world's oldest continuously operating company for some 1,400 years.[1] Think about that. For more than a dozen *centuries*, they kept busy building temples, becoming experts in their craft. And making plenty of money while doing good in the world.

Then, during the 1980s Japanese market boom, Kongō Gumi decided to expand into real estate. With uncontrolled credit access, the company took on more than $300 million in debt, and by the 1990s, the bubble had burst. Kongō Gumi was liquidated.

The company had survived countless natural disasters, great famines, political changes, world wars, and even two atomic bombs. How? By focusing. But the cause of its ultimate demise?

Losing focus.

This story is one of many that reinforces a vital fundraising tip, often ignored. Nonprofits rarely reach significant size, scale, systems change, or sustainability (which we covered in Chapter 3) without intense focus on a limited set of priorities.

You might argue that the best brands in the world do a lot of things. But these famous private-sector examples tell us that all these well-known companies focused for a long, long time before expansion:

- Apple built computers for 25 years, then came the iPod.

- McDonald's sold 1 billion burgers before adding fish.

- Google was once a $100 million search engine only.

- Virgin built a records empire, then an airline.

- Amazon started with online books.

- Nike just made running shoes.

These were all massive companies before adding additional priorities.

Now that you have your team set from the previous chapter, you must focus their efforts. Then go raise a bunch of money with these priorities. So you'll next learn how to document your priorities: **three-year picture, annual goals,** and **quarterly projects.**

*"Planning is important as a process and tool, and it informs tons of stuff. But it becomes outdated reaaaaally fast. So priorities are a good level. The art is balancing priorities (internally focused) with what you are learning from the market and the opportunities that arrive. That is the way to remain entrepreneurial, which is essential for success in a tough environment." — Leonardo Letelier, social entrepreneur (Brazil)*

# Three-year picture: painting and framing.

To start off, you need to bring the desired results from your theory of change down to earth a bit. Because your vision and 10-year target (from Chapter 3) are simply too far off to enable you to plan effectively.

There's little value in making detailed plans beyond a three-year window. But this exercise allows your team to see what you're saying. And you can more easily determine what you must do in the next 12 months to stay on track.

Measurables give everyone a better sense of scope and size. Every organization has a few very specific figures that are telltale signs of progress, impact, and growth.

This exercise is especially valuable for big-picture funder conversations — because you're painting a picture of the destination, not discussing every obstacle along the way.

## CLIENT EXAMPLE: EDUCATION PARTNERSHIPS GROUP (EPG)

- *People/presence in 10 countries.*

- *West Africa and East Africa cluster.*

- *Global thought leader, generating/sharing learning.*

- *35 people from Global South; seen as great place to work.*

- *Proven, sustainable and healthy operational business model.*

- *Independent of Ark — own identity, governance, and purpose.*

- *Three solidified practice areas, including tools and processes.*

- *Generate and guarantee a three-year funding pipeline and ~£3MM per year in unrestricted grants.*

- *Governments request for EPG assistance based on word of mouth; reduced donor word-of-mouth work.*

---

When we worked with EPG, they had a lengthy strategic plan with a bunch of TO DOs and grand visions. But nothing like this 3-year picture to help the organization (and funders) visualize what it would look like. You'll see their annual goals, based on this list, in a moment.

**ACTION STEP: LIST YOUR THREE-YEAR PICTURE**

What will your organization look like three years from now? What are the defining measurables in 8–12 bullets? For example, categories could include:

- Number of employees and lives impacted

- Additional products/services

- Awards or recognition won

- Technology innovations

- New offices/locations

- Revenue and profit

# Annual goals: 12-month priorities.

From your three-year picture, you can move into annual goals. In other words, you can determine what must get done next year. You can also consider a theme, if all of your goals roll up into a neat, singular topic (e.g., "global growth" or "African-led impact"). That sort of grouping is helpful for both you and donors alike.

Less is always more when goal setting. Social sector leaders are notorious for trying to name too many goals. Then when organizations try to cram it all in, people accomplish less and get frustrated in the process.

Leave no room for ambiguity! An outsider should be able to know what your goals mean.

Make them SMARTIE: specific, measurable, attainable, realistic, timebound, inclusive, and equitable. But we're not trying to measure these with numbers just yet — that's a few steps from now, with KPIs in Chapter 6.

## CLIENT EXAMPLE: EDUCATION PARTNERSHIPS GROUP

- *Fill all outstanding/planned staff roles by March.*

- *Publish 3–4 impact evaluations, one each quarter.*

- *Document one example of legislative or policy change by end of year.*

- *Launch new brand, website, social media, and thought leadership blog in Q2.*

- *Develop monitoring and evaluation (M&E) systems for each project, country programme, and EPG in August.*

From EPG's 3-year picture, we determined what needed to be done in the next year. It's just five big things. Because for this client, they only had about 20 people on staff — so they had to focus.

## ACTION STEP: DECIDE YOUR ANNUAL GOALS

Annual goals generally take 6–12 months to complete. And require a number of people working in subsequent quarters.

- Decide the 3–5 most important things that need to be done (or figured out) as an organization in order for it to be on track for the three-year picture.

- Annual goals need to be overarching. These are items that can serve as logical containers for quarterly projects.

- We're not yet assigning owners. That comes next in quarterly projects.

# Quarterly projects: 90-day priorities.

With annual goals in place, it's time to break the plan down further. Humans can only focus for about 90 days at a time, according to the book *Mastering the Rockefeller Habits,* by Verne Harnish. So this should be your projects cadence. Every quarter the leadership team meets to decide on the most important priorities for the next three months. All based on the annual goals.

Like goals, quarterly projects should follow the less-is-more philosophy. If everything is important, nothing is. And look, if you finish all your projects, you can add more! But it's harder to take them away once they're set, without feeling as if you're failing.

## CLIENT EXAMPLE: EDUCATION PARTNERSHIPS GROUP

- *Finalize MEL plan, incorporating revised ToC and practice areas stemming from the Strategic Working Group (Julie, January 31).*

- *Develop the Personal Development Plan for EPG staff (Faith, February 15).*

- *Finalize + embed a KPI scorecard for SMT to measure and monitor performance at SMT Meetings (Pete, February 28).*

- *Oversee the delivery of the scoping and feasibility report and PPP strategy to the Ministry of Education and British Council in Ethiopia (Rich, March 1).*

- *Finalise and embed a comprehensive database of potential funders and business opportunities that allows us to match supply and demand (Sam, March 1).*

---

As you can see after first reviewing EPG's three-year picture and annual goals above, these quarterly projects get a lot more specific — including dates and names. Most of the time these tools are not shared verbatim with funders, but they are great speaking points to prove to donors that you're making traction.

## ACTION STEP: FLESH OUT YOUR QUARTERLY PROJECTS

These projects take longer than a week but less than three months (typically 1–2 months).

- Use your three to five chosen annual goals as the guide. Under each goal, list all the projects that need to be done in the next 90 days.

- Determine the top 3–5 at the company level. Then assign one owner who is accountable for each project even if others are responsible/consulted as well. Each person on the leadership team establishes 3–5 projects of their own for the quarter. A company priority or two can make up the 3–5 personal projects.

Do you see the flow, from all the way back in your theory of change vision and 10-year target into these strategic planning priorities? Do you see why I say that your theory of change and strategic plan should be linked? And do you see why these priorities are important to show funders?

Good.

As it's now time to turn these priorities into rhythms in Chapter 6 — because goals can guide, but routines realize funding.

# Summary.

1. The priorities section of your strategic plan includes your three-year picture, annual goals, and quarterly projects. Funders really want to see this kind of plan for traction — not just a grand vision ahead.

2. You don't grow your funding *by* adding new stuff. You grow *then* add new stuff.

3. Your three-year picture begins to bring your theory of change (and 10-year target) down to earth a bit more, giving you as well as your donors the ability to see the destination.

4. Annual goals are pulled from the three-year picture, and give you a limited set of priorities you must get done in the coming 12 months.

5. Humans can only concentrate on a task for about 90 days at a time, so quarterly projects are the perfect mini-priority to set for both the organization and individual level.

# 6. RHYTHMS

## Goals can guide, but routines realize funding.

Your fundraising dreams won't make a difference. Nor will your fancy new three-year picture or brand communications plan. Not without establishing internal routines to get the strategy done.

Because raising a lot of money and then using that money well requires knowing:[1]

**How you win (or priorities, the topic of the last chapter).**

+

**How you work (or rhythms, the topic of this chapter).**

But most nonprofit leaders spend much *more* time on setting their goals and plans, and proudly telling donors about that strategy. Then they spend much *less* time ensuring that the internal team is rallied around it.

"Goals without routines are wishes; routines without goals are aimless," says the Growth Institute. And "the most successful business leaders have a clear vision and the disciplines (routines) to make it a reality."

The bottom line:

Goals guide. Routines realize funding. And plans need more than words.

So in this chapter you'll learn how to document your rhythms: **impact process, internal communications,** and **key performance indicators (KPIs).**

> *"Rhythms and rituals are key elements to keep teams focused and in momentum. Rhythms for me are the glue that holds things together when the going gets tough. And this is what a donor wants to see: you manage through a cohesive set of practices." — Dr. Güera Romo, eco-industrialist (South Africa)*

## Impact process: more cash, less chaos.

Rhythms begin with a fundraising tactic you've likely never used. But donors and teams crave it: the impact process. Because donors trust your process, not just your promise. So process isn't boring. Process is fundraising power.

Just look at the website for our friends at Spark Microgrants. This nonprofit has clearly defined and communicated its own trusted, proprietary process. In a few simple steps.

## How the Spark Process works: six key phases over the course of two years

| PHASE ONE COMMUNITY BUILDING | PHASE TWO GOAL SETTING | PHASE THREE PROPOSAL DEVELOPMENT |
|---|---|---|
| Set expectations between Spark & the community | Brainstorm & prioritize communal goals | Develop metrics for project success |
| Develop a community mission & vision | Develop objectives for reaching the top goal | Create an operational plan & budget |
| Conduct resource analysis & mapping | Research existing efforts to address each objective | Complete a risk assessment |
| Elect a leadership committee | Identify a pathway to the objective | Draft bylaws & a sustainability plan |

| PHASE FOUR TECHNICAL ADVISOR | PHASE FIVE IMPLEMENTATION | PHASE SIX FUTURE ENVISIONING |
|---|---|---|
| Receive training from a technical advisor, an outside specialist able to give expert judgment for the risk assessment & operational functionality of a specific project | Receive the micro-grant from Spark | Develop a post-Spark community plan & updated vision |
| | Enroll community members in our SMS program so they can be alerted in real time when grant disbursements are made via text message | Build partnerships with local government, NGOs & businesses |
| Revise the proposal to create a strong, quality project plan | Launch their project | Independently manage their project |

FIGURE 8: The Spark Process, re-created as an illustration.

This brand tactic can maximize your own funding in two ways:

**Revenue (more cash** *externally*): It gives donors faith you can pull off your theory of change. Thus, you generate more top-line revenue via fundraising.

**Efficiency (less chaos** *internally*): It gives teams a repeatable roadmap to execute efficiently. Thus, you drive more impact and bottom-line profit despite limited resources.

Why does this brand tactic work?

Well, classic storytelling frameworks teach us that funders, customers, and teams only trust a guide — and a story — with a process. Imagine you're on a guided hike through a dense jungle. You're scared as you reach a raging river. But your tour guide says, "We'll cross the river by stepping on this safe rock, that big log, then these dry stones. Don't worry, I do it every day."

So you cross. But without your guide explaining the process, you likely wouldn't.

It's such a simple and valuable fundraising tactic. And surprisingly rare. Most nonprofits don't have an impact process to begin with. If they do, it's unused by the team and it's certainly not shared with the outside world.

This impact process has been a lightbulb moment for our clients. Give it a try and watch the magic happen.

Because your mission deserves a method.

**ACTION STEP: DOCUMENT YOUR PROCESSES**

Identify and list the 2–3 most important processes that drive your organization.

- Name each process. And decide if you want the process to be better, faster, or cheaper (which are the only three ways to improve it).

- Assign someone specific accountability for each core process.

- Then for each process, list out the 5–10 major steps required (in a couple of words!) with arrows in between. Not all the little details along the way. A graphic illustration is even better.

# Internal comms: aligning your brand within your team.

Your marketing communications are critical, of course. But most nonprofits lack big brand budgets, which means they have a limited ability to use channels and media to reach new donors.

But one thing every nonprofit has? A team full of people. Speaking and meeting every day, inside and outside the organization. Hopefully communicating a compelling story about your brand to both funders and partners.

Let's use One Acre Fund as a hypothetical. This unicorn nonprofit has grown to $250 million in revenue across seven countries with some 8,000 staff. If everyone on the team speaks with 10 people a day, that's 21 million (!) messaging opportunities a year from the most important brand ambassadors: internal staff.

You might not be at 8,000 people in size like One Acre Fund, but the math still proves the point. If your leaders can't get your message across clearly and motivate your own team, then having a message doesn't even matter.

> *"The single biggest problem in communication is the illusion that it has taken place."* — George Bernard Shaw, playwright (Ireland)

Research by Gartner shows that 70% of business mistakes are due to poor internal communication rhythms. And according to Gallup, 74% of employees feel they're missing out on company information and news. So tell me how it's possible to build a brand from the inside out with this type of lack of communication?

## Your team should be mocking you.

Seriously. Because you repeat the same message. Over and over and over again.

Repetition is not the same as micro-management. That's telling people *how* to do their jobs. Over-communication is reinforcing *why* their work matters, *who* is responsible, *what* they should be doing, *when* it needs to be done, and *where* the organization is going in the future.

It's part and parcel of good leadership.

And a solid internal communication rhythm helps you in a dozen ways, according to the Nonprofit Marketing Guide:

- Motivate staff to act.

- Foster accountability.

- Streamline workflows.

- Boost decision making.

- Create brand ambassadors.

- Build relationships and trust.

- Improve project coordination.

- Unify people around shared goals.

- Align and update priorities as needed.

- Encourage more listening and learning.

- Provide big-picture context for decisions.

- Implement changes within the organization.

… all of which leads to maximized funding. Because you're operating more efficiently and also making the most of the fundraising you receive. If you're with me, what do you think is the key to effective over-communication?

Well, there are countless digital tools for team chats, staff input, stakeholder feedback, and performance dashboards. But the key to great internal comms (and great internal rhythms) is largely this: consistently getting together as a team and then passionately discussing what's important. Yes, meetings. And meeting *well*. The problem isn't that meetings are terrible. It's that we're terrible at running them (that's why there are countless books on that specific topic).

You need meetings to repeat, repeat, repeat the same core messaging. Repeat, repeat, repeat your same theory of change, positioning strategy, and strategic plan. Every channel, every conversation. Rhythms, rhythms, rhythms.

Again and again until it sticks.

So be a beacon — repeating your rays of organizational clarity.

And "over-communicate," advises author Alex Irvine. "It's better to tell someone something they already know than to not tell them something they needed to hear."

Because brand isn't a solo act. It's an orchestra. Rhythms unify every voice and every note.

*"Great leadership is about connecting with others and creating a sense of confidence and [teamwork]. None of this happens without exceptional communication skills, which involves more than giving a great speech." — Steve Adubato, author (United States)*

Use a simple text list to decide with your leadership team on your internal comms rhythms. Then book recurring calendar invitations in advance. Some ideas to get you started:

- **Meetings:** Department daily standups and monthly one-on-ones; leadership weekly, quarterly, and annual; quarterly town hall.

- **Tools:** Staff engagement surveys; monthly CEO letter to the full team; a guide for resolving issues.

# Key performance indicators (KPIs): leading and lagging.

Nonprofits often obsess over impact data. It's great to build monitoring and evaluation systems to measure the success of external programs. But rarely do we see the same obsession with the success of the internal organization itself.

That's where leaders must shift from working *in* the business to *on* the business, so as to ensure long-term fundraising viability.

(Think back to what I shared earlier: a major family foundation told me they don't invest if they doubt the organization can execute its idea. And KPIs are one big signal whether you're executing or not.)

It's nearly impossible to achieve a vision or raise much money without setting and hitting KPIs. Let's break it down a bit more.

*"All data is wrong. Some are useful."* — *Unknown*

## Setting KPIs.

There are two types of KPIs: lagging and leading. Both are critical, and you shouldn't use one without the other.

*Lagging KPIs* are all about measuring what's already happened — the output metrics that tell you how your organization performed during a time when it's too late to do anything about it. Think basic organizational stats: donations, sales, the number of government partners, or team growth.

To determine your lagging KPIs, list the key results you'd flaunt in an investor pitch or annual report. You might brainstorm a dozen or more, but let's get real: focus on 6–10 that truly matter, then track them relentlessly.

## CLIENT EXAMPLE: CORNER TO CORNER

- *New hires*

- *Event reviews*

- *Academy participants*

- *New project successes*

- *Total annual giving to date*

---

This faith-based nonprofit working with Black entrepreneurs in Nashville (United States) was growing rapidly when we led their strategic planning process. And the new leadership team needed to gather each quarter to keep their eye on the most important internal and financial KPIs.

---

## ACTION STEP: SET YOUR QUARTERLY KPIS

The best way to determine lagging KPIs is to list the most important results you'd put in an annual report.

- Pick the top 6–10 to measure each quarter. These are typically at the organizational, performance metrics level — not M&E impact metrics on the ground.

- Select a quarterly target.

- Create a basic dashboard that you'll review every 90 days.

On the other hand, *leading KPIs* are your crystal ball — they're the input metrics that predict whether you're on track to crush your goals. Done right, they give you a glimpse into the future, going beyond the typical numbers on a quarterly report.

Think of metrics like the number of funder meetings held or the count of staff complaints. These are your early warning systems.

(A personal example that shows the difference between the two: if your *lagging* indicator is finishing a marathon in under three hours, some *leading* indicators might include running 80km/week for the months prior or stretching for 15 mins every night.)

Money talks, and leading KPIs make sure you're always in the conversation. Without them, you could end the quarter with your fundraising off target and no time to recover.

Leading KPIs show you the trends early, giving you a chance to tweak your strategy and keep the donations rolling in, long before looking at the final tally.

## CLIENT EXAMPLE: CORNER TO CORNER

- *New grants received*

- *New first-time donors*

- *High-net-worth touchpoints*

- *Number of email subscribers*

- *Academy applications received*

---

Based on the quarterly, lagging KPIs list shared above, our client determined this set of leading KPIs that the leadership team would watch week to week. As you can see, most of these weekly measures focused on fundraising.

## ACTION STEP: PICK YOUR WEEKLY KPIS

If you were on a desert island, think about the most important metrics that would tell you that your organization (onshore) is performing well.

- To determine leading KPIs (tracked weekly), take your 6–10 lagging KPIs. Then come up with a list of the most critical activities that must happen every week in order to hit your quarterly targets.

- Pick the top 12–15, and fill out a scorecard you can review every week.

- Assign an owner for each leading KPI.

Congrats, you've completed the entire strategic planning section. And you're done with Part One, which helps you become fundable before findable.

Up next is Part Two: Be Findable.

# Summary.

1. The rhythms section of your strategic plan includes impact process, internal communications, and KPIs.

2. Setting goals or even priorities isn't enough. Real change comes from focusing on the intersection of: how you win (priorities) + how you work (rhythms).

3. An impact process is one of the most undervalued tactics for maximized funding, as it leads to more fundraising wins, plus making the most of the money you receive.

4. Internal communications doesn't get as much attention as do marketing communications, but it can help you in at least a dozen ways.

5. Setting and tracking KPIs — both leading and lagging — is how you measure organizational performance (different from impact monitoring and evaluation).

# PART TWO:
# BE FINDABLE

Occupying a distinct space in the minds of your ideal funders, and routinely communicating your promises to them.

# Friendly warning.

Did you buy this book and immediately skip ahead to this Part Two: Be Findable section? You sneaky rascal. Or did you recently complete Part One: Be Fundable? And you're excited to keep going? Well, that's awesome but... let's pause for a quick gut check to see if your brand is on its way to being *fundable* yet. Because you must remember the sequence: more fundraising can't fix your fundraising. To get funding, be fundable and findable (brand first).

I'll give you 10 brief statements. These statements cover what you should have understood by reading Part One. So now you can rank your organization on a scale of 1 to 5 for each statement, where 1 is *weak/don't know* and 5 is *strong*.

## Theory of change.

- We have a theory of change in writing that's shared inside and outside the organization — especially with funders.

- We can articulate the need that fuels our work, including the problem statement, people served, and reason for being.

- We know how to communicate various elements of the work with donors, including inputs, interventions, partners, big idea, and mission.

- Our messaging to funders includes the results we're trying to create — pathways, outputs, outcomes, 10-year target, and vision.

- Our theory of change drives decisions in related areas like fundraising, M&E, staffing, and partnerships.

## Strategic plan.

- Our staff has the right people in the right seats — based on core values — with the capacity to achieve the vision.

- We have documented and shared publicly impact processes — based on the theory of change — that build trust and credibility with donors.

- An active strategic plan aids in our fundraising and guides yearly, quarterly, and weekly priorities that are tied to our three-year picture.

- Our organization has good internal communications rhythms, as evidenced by team alignment, effective meetings, and resolving issues well.

- We can back up our brand story with funders or investors via data, like leading activity scorecards and lagging KPI dashboards.

# How to assess your scores.

Total your points, then divide by 10 to get your average. Our clients average a 3 out of 5 for the questions above. And honestly, their strategic planning scores are slightly lower. Higher scores often equal higher funding.

Still, the goal is a 4.5. That's just 90% in school grade terms. We're not even aiming for a perfect 5.0 or 100%. So if you're not there yet, read on about being findable, but keep putting in the efforts to be fundable, first. Because being fundable will help you raise far more money than any flashy marketing campaign.

Fair?

Now that I've made my point — off the soapbox — let's continue into Part Two. It begins with your positioning strategy.

P.S. — Before we dive into Part Two, take a moment to recognize your commitment to this process. You've shown up, read page by page, and tackled every exercise to get through Part One.

By this point, you should feel comfortable showing donors why you exist, what you do, who will do it, where you're going, how to get there, and when it will be done. The rest of the advice in this book won't take you as far without having laid this foundation.

So you're now halfway to the promise I made you in the beginning: that you'll have the understanding and framework to build a clear, compelling nonprofit brand that maximizes your funding and advances social justice. Maybe when you first opened this book, you didn't expect to wield this level of skill. Now? You're holding it. Own that.

And keep pushing forward.

# POSITIONING STRATEGY

Distinguish your brand and break through the noise in the minds of donors with this blueprint.

Imagine a grocery store aisle full of green apples. Hundreds of them. Can you visualize it?

Right in the middle is a single red apple.

Which apple got your attention? Easy. Now, which one is the best quality? Debatable. That's why *different* beats *better*. Because being a unique brand is objective. Different is hard to argue. But being a superior brand is subjective. Better is in the eye of the beholder.

Being distinct from your competitors speaks for itself. You can use short, punchy communications. But being greater than those competitors requires explanation. You need lengthy messaging and marketing.

Ideally, you're both different *and* better. Especially in the social sector — where lives are on the line — accountable products and programs are paramount for the communities we serve. Although, assuming you're already creating impact, nobody will know you're the best or better nonprofit if you don't stand out in the crowd.

If you're the red apple in that grocery aisle, donors notice you. You gain that funder meeting. It's not guaranteed that you will land the investment. But at least you have a shot to tell your story.

Unlike the many green apples — they're lost in the noise. Because most nonprofits endlessly talk about how they're better.

Let this resonate:

> *"It's not enough to be the best at what you do. You must be perceived as the only one who does what you do."*
> — *Jerry Garcia, musician (United States)*

So, in a world with some 10 million nonprofits, if many other organizations can say the same things — your brand is not unique enough. You may in fact be better. Perhaps even the best. But it's not the same as being different. Don't be the best. Be the only.[1]

How? Determine your positioning strategy. That's how. It's a process that, when landed, can sharpen everything you do — from programs to fundraising.

In this section, you'll learn more about positioning strategy: **what it is, why it matters,** and **how to create one.** Then you'll fully unpack the three main parts of positioning in Chapters 7, 8, and 9.

> *"As your own best salesperson, you may clearly grasp the nuances of your work. But outsiders can't readily identify a real difference, one from the other."* — *Kathleen Souder, Mighty Ally Founding Partner (Ireland)*

# What it is.

Positioning strategy is all about boldly claiming your strengths, finding the gaps where others are missing, and presenting your brand with clarity and confidence. It's not just about entering the marketplace; it's making a statement that donors can't ignore.

Nonprofits juggle two markets: those they serve and those who fund them. One side is about connecting with participants or customers. The other? Capturing the attention of funders, partners, and sector influencers. The strategies laid out below work for both markets. But remember, this book focuses mostly on winning over those who hold the purse strings.

Here's a helpful mental model in Figure 9 to better understand positioning, conceived by my Founding Partner Kathleen Souder:

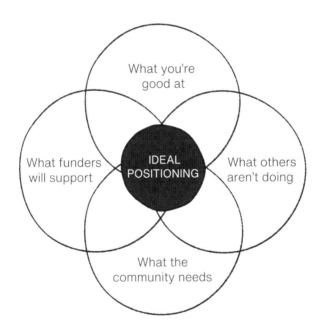

FIGURE 9: Positioning strategy sweet spot.[2]

Need a tangible example of positioning in action? Let's compare three cancer nonprofits with similar missions and visions in their theories of change. But with radically different positioning.

The Susan G. Komen Foundation: feminine, active, positive. Fuck Cancer: young, rebellious, angry. American Cancer Society: academic, trusted, corporate.

Even by their names alone you get a sense of how they're positioned. And with just one glance at their visuals (go take a look at their websites) you'll see immediately who they're for and who they're not.

# Why it matters: maximized funding.

Without sharp positioning, your message will get lost in the crowd. Your team's focus will fade, and crucial opportunities for collaboration will pass you by, weakening your impact. Ultimately, good positioning strategy allows you to maximize your funding.

It maximizes funding in three ways:

### Attract and increase donor awareness.

Funders and donors aren't customers. Though they still want value in exchange for their investment. So you must make a strong case for why money should be given to *you* instead of someone else (in other words, how/why you're different). Of course, philanthropic giving isn't a zero-sum game. Yet your organization's ability to garner additional donors or increase donation amounts demands a clearly articulated — and differentiated — value proposition.

## Focus and align internal teams.

Positioning strategy requires you to highlight the parts of your organization that are unique and important externally. But the ability to tell that clear, compelling story first requires razor-sharp internal clarity on these factors.

To be clear, positioning isn't done for organizational performance. However, if you identify the unique value you provide, a natural next step is orienting teams and internal processes toward said value. This alignment makes the most of the funding you receive.

## Find collaboration and partnership opportunities.

Positioning will help you see areas of your work that other organizations are already doing. That visibility can help you decide if your resources could be better spent finding collaborative partners, so that you can focus instead on your big idea (remember Chapter 2?). In some cases, teaming up with another organization could help secure funding by making you stronger than you could have been on your own.

A good example is the partnership between Living Goods and Last Mile Health which won the $50 million Audacious Prize. Both organizations have theories of change centered around delivering healthcare in hard-to-reach locales using community health workers (CHWs). The project's success relies, at least in part, on the overlap of experience in deploying teams of CHWs. Living Goods supplies a Smart Health app and home delivery model, while Last Mile Health's Community Health Academy powers the workers' education.

# How to create your positioning strategy.

Positioning is an art. And it's not always easy to bull's-eye the intersection between internal realities and the external environment.

Nailing it requires equal measures of soul-searching, research, intuition, rigorous analysis, practical experience, and creativity. You'll determine your positioning strategy in three big parts. Here's the high-level summary:

**Landscape:** Coming up in Chapter 7, you'll look at your SWOT (strengths, weaknesses, opportunities, and threats), plus competitor analysis.

**Value propositions:** In Chapter 8, you will document your uniques, audiences, personas, and brand promises.

**Brand personality:** To wrap up positioning, in Chapter 9 you will establish a visual and verbal feeling through your brand character, traits, and tradition.

As with the theory of change and strategic plan, you can distill a positioning strategy into a blueprint like the one in Figure 10. It's an invaluable reference point to keep your team aligned.

And some quick encouragement here. Truly, no nonprofit we've ever worked with had a full positioning strategy already in place. So if some of these concepts feel a bit foreign to you, they should. But I promise it's not only doable. It's a must.

The best way to test your new positioning? Put it out in the real world. Learn, adapt, and then refine. Embrace design thinking to stay in tune with shifting needs and competitors. Plant your stake boldly, but always stay agile and ready to pivot.

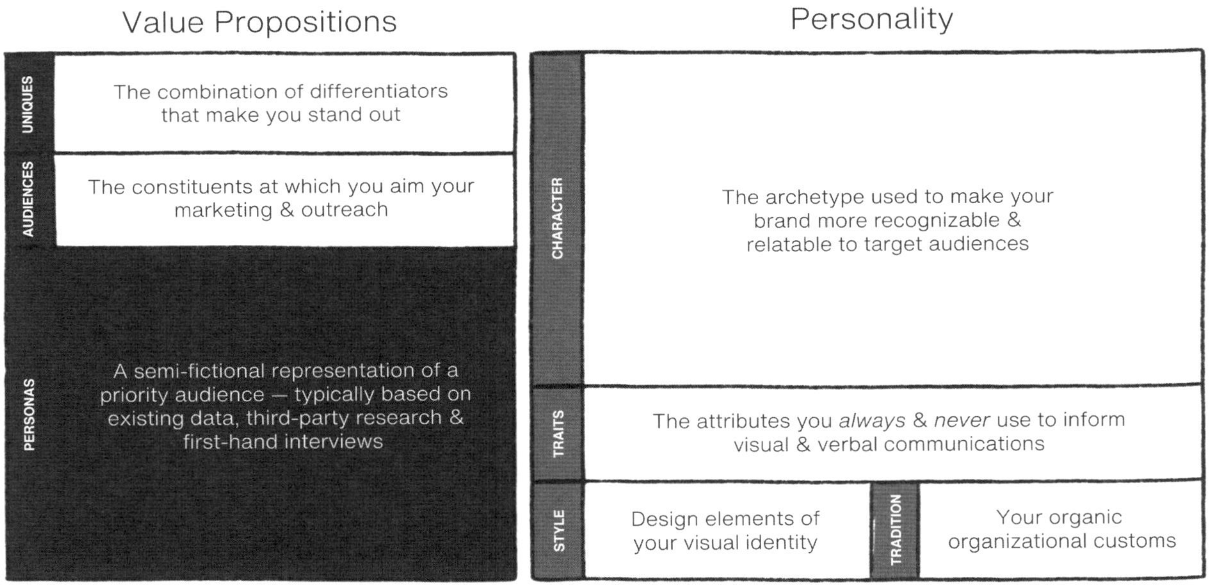

# Value Propositions

**UNIQUES**
The combination of differentiators that make you stand out

**AUDIENCES**
The constituents at which you aim your marketing & outreach

**PERSONAS**
A semi-fictional representation of a priority audience — typically based on existing data, third-party research & first-hand interviews

# Personality

**CHARACTER**
The archetype used to make your brand more recognizable & relatable to target audiences

**TRAITS**
The attributes you *always* & *never* use to inform visual & verbal communications

**STYLE**
Design elements of your *visual* identity

**TRADITION**
Your organic organizational customs

FIGURE 10: The Mighty Ally positioning strategy blueprint.[3]

## Find your lanes, find your funding.

Before we move on, I want to help you determine when to position yourself *more* and when you might be narrowing too much.

Because everyone in the business says to find a lane and stick with it. But I disagree. A single lane doesn't in fact lead to the strongest brand and strongest fundraising. Instead, find the intersection of 2–3 well-moving lanes. And upgrade from *good* to *better* to *best* positioning.

Like these example nonprofit niches:

- Education (**good**)

- Education + girls (**better**)

- Education + girls + secondary (**best**)


- Mental health (**good**)

- Mental health + refugees (**better**)

- Mental health + refugees + children (**best**)


- Smallholder farmers (**good**)

- Smallholder farmers + India (**better**)

- Smallholder farmers + India + greenhouses (**best**)

That's how you move right to left from *Undifferentiated* to *Ideal* in Figure 11.

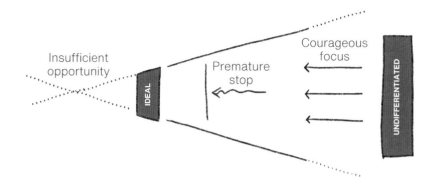

FIGURE 11: From undifferentiated to ideal positioning. Credit: David C. Baker.[4]

There's a risk in differentiating too far though. Because you'll find *Insufficient Opportunity* for funding on the far left, as seen in this illustration. Like if you focused too narrowly on smallholder farmers + India + greenhouses + girls.

But honestly, most nonprofits struggle with the other side of the graphic: *Courageous Focus.*

So, don't be afraid. To find your ideal positioning, avoid the jammed highways of undifferentiated organizations. Pick the side streets. And dare to take the road less traveled. The riches are in the niches.

Narrow lanes, wider funds.

That's how you create a category of your own. And that's how you captivate donors. So — now that you have a sense of what positioning is and why it matters — it's time to dig into the details. Let's look at your Landscape, up next in Chapter 7.

# Summary.

1. A good positioning strategy consists of the following three parts: landscape, value propositions, and brand personality.

2. Positioning strategy is a concept born in the private sector, but applies to nonprofits just as much (if not more) due to the number of similar organizations.

3. Strive to be the *only*, instead of the best. Because quality is debatable, but uniqueness is objective.

4. Ideal positioning is the perfect intersection of *what you're good at* + *what other organizations aren't doing* + *what funders will support* + *what your community needs*.

5. Strong positioning can help you in many ways, including increased fundraising, better-focused internal teams, and finding collaboration/partnership opportunities.

# 7. LANDSCAPE
You're competing for story instead of glory.

Nonprofit competition isn't an evil, capitalist sin. And it doesn't require winning at the cost of another. Because *to compete* simply means "the process of trying to get something that someone else is also trying to get," according to the Britannica Dictionary.

So, like it or not, nonprofits have competition.

Your brand is one of many options. Think about all your audiences: media, donors, volunteers, customers, foundations, corporations, NGO partners, board members, industry influencers, government officials, and even participants.

You compete in some way for their time, fundraising, sales, MOUs, awards, speaker lists, influence, inbox attention, social media algorithms, and so on.

Even inaction is a competitor. Such as a donor spending $10 on a Starbucks latte instead of giving that money to you. Or a program officer getting distracted by TikTok rather than reading your grant application. Or a community member deciding to wait for another nonprofit intervention.

Get this.

There are actually three *benefits* to nonprofit competition,[1] says social entrepreneur Tori Utley:

**Competition creates capacity:** More nonprofits in the same field mean more people served.

**Competition fosters innovation:** We're forced to stay motivated, stay unique, and stay on top of our game.

**Competition keeps us accountable:** When other options exist, we must prove how/why we're better.

> *"Collaborate when you can, compete when you must, and innovate constantly, for the good of the cause and the people you're serving." — Tori Utley, social entrepreneur (United States)*

The central idea here:

It doesn't matter if your model is one-of-a-kind and you're working in a place others aren't. It doesn't matter if the nonprofit idealist in you bristles at the concept of competition. And it doesn't matter that there should be plenty of money to go around.

You're not competing for *glory*. But you still must position your organization — in the minds of your audiences — amidst every other nonprofit in the world.

So you're competing for *story*.

Differentiation starts by looking at your landscape: an essential precursor to positioning. It reveals what's realistic within your organization, as well as what outside players are already doing. So in this chapter you'll learn how to determine your **SWOT** and your **competitor analysis.**

## SWOT: investigating, inside and out.

Information about your organization's internal capabilities and external environment is crucial to informing your positioning strategy and ensuring that you make the right fundraising decisions.

That's why the classic SWOT chart (strengths, weaknesses, opportunities, and threats)[2] is also an important tool for uncovering opportunities in your operations.

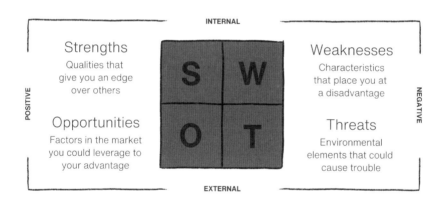

FIGURE 12: A classic SWOT analysis tool.

## ACTION STEP: DETERMINE YOUR STRENGTHS

Internal qualities that give you an edge over others.

- What do people say you do best?

- What are your strongest assets today?

- What unique resources can you access for the future?

- What skills do your employees have that others do not?

- Why should you — of all organizations — undertake this mission?

## ACTION STEP: NAME YOUR WEAKNESSES

Internal characteristics that place you at a disadvantage.

- What could you improve?

- What complaints do you regularly hear?

- Why shouldn't you undertake this mission?

- In what areas are competitors better than you?

- What expertise, knowledge, or skills do you lack?

## ACTION STEP: LIST YOUR OPPORTUNITIES

External factors you could leverage to your advantage.

- What is missing in the market?

- Is there a niche you're not currently targeting?

- Which/what partners can support you, and how?

- What trends might positively affect your industry?

- Is your target market changing in a way that could help?

## ACTION STEP: NAME YOUR THREATS

Environmental elements that could cause trouble.

- Is your target market or funding shrinking?

- What if a natural or political disaster strikes?

- What about incumbent or insurgent competitors?

- Are competitors planning on expanding offerings soon?

- Are there standards, policies, and/or legislation ahead?

# Competitor analysis: common ground.

Beyond the basic SWOT, a competitor analysis tool can be invaluable to help identify gaps and noise in your market.

On the positive side, funders are requiring more cooperation than ever before, which dictates that you gain a solid understanding of potential collaborators too.

Once you fill out a grid like Figure 13, what will likely emerge — among the noise — are opportunities and value propositions your organization can fully claim. You'll start to identify your uniques that, when combined, should elicit one compelling market position.

| | Competitor | Competitor | Competitor | Competitor | Competitor | Competitor | YOUR ORG |
|---|---|---|---|---|---|---|---|
| Attribute | X | X | X | | X | | X |
| "Based in Africa" | | / | / | / | | / | X |
| "Focuses on WASH" | | | | | | | X |
| "Earned revenue stream" | | | | | | | X |
| Attribute | | | | | | | / |
| Attribute | | | | | | | |
| Attribute | | | | | | | X |
| Attribute | | | | | | | / |
| Attribute | | | | | | | |
| Attribute | | | | | | | / |

FIGURE 13: A competitor/peer/landscape analysis grid.

**ACTION STEP: FILL OUT YOUR COMPETITOR ANALYSIS**

Use a simple Excel or Google Sheets grid, like Figure 13, to analyze other organizations in your space.

- List all current and potential competitors across the top. These are names of other organizations.

- Down the side, list all the factors or qualities you want to compare. These are characteristics that might be important to your donors.

- Then mark an X where a competitor meets that factor, mark a half / (slash) where they somewhat do, and leave blank factors they don't.

- Finally, chart your own organization on the far right.

Then look for gaps and noise!

## Where two brands collide, fundraising thrives.

When thinking about your competitors, collaborators, and landscape, here's a telling and fun positioning tool for your team:

If brands had babies, what would your mix be? Gather your team and try to answer this question:

> **We're like if BRAND X and BRAND Y had a baby.**

We do this exercise with clients in our positioning strategy workshop. And it helps generate daring and memorable combinations, such as:

- We're like if Uber and John Deere had a baby — connecting tractor owners to smallholder farmers in need.

- Think of us as Spotify meets Harvard — providing free, unlimited online learning for underprivileged students.

- We're a mix of BYD plus Habitat for Humanity — revolutionizing affordable, eco-friendly housing in urban slums.

You might not decide to share your baby combination with the outside world. It could just remain an internal, strategic exercise to drive comms clarity. And spark new ideas.

Yet successful brand builders often position their organizations by comparing themselves to giants in other fields.

This is because using a well-known company reduces the cognitive load for your audience. Funders can more easily understand your model if they already have a mental image of the reference brands. Plus, these comparisons can be unique conversation starters — sparking curiosity and inviting questions about your work.

Give it a try. You may be surprised at the answers that emerge. So, what's your unique brand child?

Once you have that answer (that brand baby), you'll be ready to tell the world about where you fit in it. And that's the topic of Chapter 8, which focuses on value propositions.

# Summary.

1.  The landscape section of your positioning strategy contains your SWOT and competitor analysis.

2.  Whether you like it or not, you compete in some way with every other nonprofit in the world and, frankly, with everything else in the world.

3.  Nonprofit competition can actually be good, because it creates capacity, fosters innovation, and keeps us accountable.

4.  A SWOT analysis gives you a valuable precursor to positioning because it ensures that you're fully aware of both internal and external realities.

5.  A competitor analysis enables you to line up your organization next to others, compare attributes, and find the gaps (where others aren't) and noise (where probably many others are).

# 8. VALUE PROPOSITIONS

## Difference = donations. Emphasize it.

Fundraising secret? Three crucial words:

*How we're different.*

Let me explain.

Donors are wired for comparison. To make sense of a complicated world, the human brain uses reference points as a cognitive shortcut. Especially since there's a lot (lot) of overlap in the social sector — with many (many) nonprofits doing the same thing. In the same places, even.

This nonprofit overlap and these mental comparisons can lead to preconceived donor doubt. Funders think:

"Yet another water charity."

"Yet another climate nonprofit."

"Yet another teacher training model."

So once a donor understands the problem you solve, what you do, and where you're going — always start with that theory of change! — hit them next with your differentiators.

Uniqueness sells.

"The goal is not to fit in," says music producer Rick Rubin.[1] "If anything, it's to amplify the differences, what doesn't fit, the special characteristics unique to how you see the world."

Even just say in your conversations with potential funders, *there are a lot of great organizations in this space, but here's how we're different.* This confident statement bolsters your credibility and increases interest. It demonstrates that you respect your peers, but have built a better mousetrap.

With your landscape analysis completed in the previous chapter, the next step is to take that intelligence and make some key decisions around the value you promise to deliver.

So in this value propositions chapter, you'll learn how to determine your **uniques, audiences (including five donor options), personas,** and **brand promises.**

## Uniques: what makes you different.

Also known as differentiators, these uniques are what make your organization stand out from the rest in the minds of your funders.

> *"Most nonprofits in my country set themselves up for failure. They copy and paste causes, visions, strategies, or activities from their competition who they believe have made it. And yet they cannot articulate or translate their differences well to the donor. So donors see through the lies, and hold back funding." — Stella Nassuna, multimedia professional (Uganda)*

Here's the tricky part: any organization can identify and claim differentiators. But uniques that also truly matter to your audiences? Uniques that solve a key problem? That's a lot harder.

## CLIENT EXAMPLES

*Transform Schools*

- *Exclusive secondary focus*
- *Scale with partnerships across the whole state system*
- *High-ROI, shared-cost funding model with the Indian government*

*Food for Education*

- *African-led*
- *Tech-enabled*
- *Nutrient-dense meals from verified safe kitchens*

*Pace Able Foundation*

- *Hands-on advisory*
- *Start-up expertise*
- *Servant leadership*

---

In all three cases, we've not yet crafted public-facing messaging around these uniques (that comes in the messaging and storytelling chapter). But these are short-hand decisions the teams made to help position their brand uniquely.

**ACTION STEP: DECIDE ON YOUR UNIQUES**

Start by looking back at the SWOT analysis and competitor grid we covered in Chapter 7. In your SWOT, are there strengths that others don't have? Be sure to avoid the weaknesses here. Now look at the gaps in the landscape analysis for where you shine and others don't. Then list the three greatest factors/elements that make you truly unique. They must be:

- Authentic

- Important to priority audiences

- Provable

# Audiences: speak to the relevant few.

Also known as a target market, a priority audience is a specific group of constituents at which your organization aims its brand. In many cases, these audiences are different from your beneficiaries or participants (remember the people element Chapter 1).

No one can afford to target everyone. In fact, pick just three audiences. And resist the urge to be generic in order to go after a larger slice of the market. The equivalent in archery would be lobbing 10 arrows in random directions instead of aiming just one at the center of the bull's-eye. Defining audiences can help you streamline your fundraising efforts, plus maximize your marketing communications budget.

## CLIENT EXAMPLES

*Lwala*

- *Advanced institutional funders*
- *Peer collaborators*
- *Kenyan partners*

*Nyaka*

- *Low- and mid-tier family foundations*
- *High-net-worth individuals*
- *Individual donors*

*STiR Education*

- *High-level government officials*
- *Mid-level government officials*
- *International influencers*

What I love about these three client examples is how different they are. Lwala was going upstream in its donor targets, and also needed to reach peers with its brand. Nyaka defined three different types of funders, because just saying your brand is for donors isn't specific enough. And STiR Education was so intent on reaching government officials, they actually split this audience into two: because the messaging and media would be drastically different between a ministry-level official and a local official.

**ACTION STEP: DETERMINE YOUR AUDIENCES**

List your top three targets in order of importance (like donors, government, or beneficiaries).

- Identify the ideal geographic, demographic, and psychographic characteristics of each audience.

- Describe each audience with 1–2 sentences.

- Keep in mind these are audiences for the brand, not necessarily for those communities you serve.

# Right donors, right fit: your five options.

For those of you completely new to fundraising and donor audiences, here's a quick breakdown of your five donor options.[2]

Each of the five categories has its donor motivations, advantages and constraints for you, plus capabilities that you need internally to attract and retain those funders. So it's going to be nearly impossible to reach and engage all of them with a single brand.

| DONOR TYPE | DONOR MOTIVATIONS | ADVANTAGES FOR YOU | CONSTRAINTS FOR YOU | CAPABILITIES YOU NEED |
|---|---|---|---|---|
| Governments | Provide essential services to constituents<br><br>Federal funders often prefer replicable projects & third-party evals<br><br>State & local funders often look for evidence of community support | Can provide predictable contracts over a defined period with the potential to renew<br><br>Most frequent, major funding source for nonprofits with $50M+ in annual revenue | Often restricted & may cap overhead rates<br><br>Application process & reporting requirements can be extensive<br><br>Payment often comes after service delivery | Lobbying & government relations<br><br>Technical grant writing on RFPs & proposals<br><br>Contracting<br><br>Compliance & reporting |
| Corporations | Create ties between the corp's brand & a meaningful social cause<br><br>Motivate employees with volunteering & gift matching | Often contribute in-kind goods, services, or pro bono time<br><br>Can provide access to additional donors via customers or employees | Often establish new priorities, so current grantmaking gets scaled back or discontinued<br><br>Need to balance business & philanthropic goals | Branding, marketing & communications<br><br>Board members with corporate connections<br><br>Employee volunteer opportunities |
| High-net-worths | Build individual &/or family legacy<br><br>Find meaning & joy in deploying wealth to worthy causes<br><br>Invest in a personal interest or passion<br><br>Maximize tax benefits | Can be nimble at times, with the potential to make efficient decisions on large gifts<br><br>May facilitate introductions to other major donors | Fundraising is idiosyncratic & priorities may change<br><br>Hard to access without existing relationships<br><br>Can require high-touch engagement from senior leaders | Connections to wealthy individuals<br><br>Board of directors committed to fundraising & willing to make introductions<br><br>Major gift stewardship & solicitation |
| Foundations | Invest in sectors & geographies that align with the foundation's mission & strategy<br><br>Achieve something distinctive over an extended timeline | Program officers often have deep knowledge of social impact topics<br><br>Foundations often learn from one another & share ideas, creating a network effect | Typically accessed by invite only; do not take inbound inquiries<br><br>Often restricted & may cap overhead<br><br>Can establish new priorities, leading to shifts in funding | Technical grant writing<br><br>Connections to program officers at foundations<br><br>Monitoring, evaluation & reporting |
| Small gifts | Contribute to a well-known cause, often in response to social media or mail campaigns<br><br>Respond to urgent needs, like natural disasters<br><br>Maximize tax benefits | Typically unrestricted<br><br>Highly diversified; a multitude of relationships with small donors means less reliance on any single donor | Donor acquisition cost can be high relative to small gift size<br><br>Can experience high turnover in donors each year | Strong brand awareness & widespread appeal<br><br>Marketing, such as digital ads & mail campaigns<br><br>Payment infrastructure |

FIGURE 14: Donor types, motivations, advantages, constraints, and capabilities.

# Personas: get up close and personal.

The priority audience we just covered is a broad representation of your target market. Now, taking it a step further, developing a persona for each audience allows for a much deeper understanding of that target at a human level.

A persona is a semi-fictional representation of a priority audience — typically based off existing data, third-party research, and first-hand interviews.

You'll use an empathy map[3] which is simply a framework to better understand (and empathize with!) each persona.

The saying goes "it's what's inside that counts" — meaning, a constituent's thoughts and feelings typically affect what they say and do.

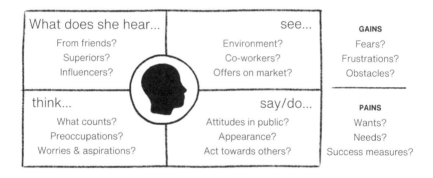

FIGURE 15: A personas empathy map tool.

## ACTION STEP: EMPATHIZE WITH AUDIENCES

Develop one empathy map for each of your three audiences. Take notes on everything you know about them:

- What are his *pains*: Fears, frustrations, obstacles?

- What are her *gains*: Wants, needs, success measures?

- What does he *hear*: From friends, superiors, influencers?

- What does she *see*: Environment, co-workers, offers on market?

- What does he *say/do*: Attitude in public, appearance, act toward others?

- What does she *think*: What counts, preoccupations, worries and aspirations?

## You might not know your customers well enough.

As you get started on your personas, let me tell you a quick story. Our second-ever client was an agriculture distribution social enterprise in Colombia. They had an innovative solution, a talented team, World Bank research, and prestigious funding.

But they were about to go under.

This is an example about the need to have empathy with your audiences. It's also an example of how not every one of your brand audiences must be fundraising-related. For some of you, you're also reaching customers or even participants with your brand.

We at Mighty Ally went into the agricultural engagement in Colombia, thinking it was a marketing challenge: communicating that their delivery service saved Mom-and-Pop *tenderos* (store owners) hours of transport time.

Turns out, the social enterprise just didn't understand its customers. Turns out, the leaders had spent far too much time in the office (too much time on fundraising and operations), and far too little time in the field. Turns out, the tenderos actually *wanted to* travel to the central market every morning — as it was their only social activity of the day.

So the entire business model had been built on a flimsy premise. On a flimsy brand. And by the time we surfaced this game-changing insight, it was indeed too late. The company failed.

So what significant insight are you missing from your funder or participant audiences? Go find out. Keep finding out.

And continually ask yourself: in designing the bridge, are we thinking about the people who will cross it? Your brand success could hinge on this knowledge gap.

> "*When building and scaling an enterprise, it is absolutely crucial to make customer discovery an ongoing practice. While many companies have built great feedback loops with their customers (which is important), this is different. It is indispensable to engage with current, future and ex-customers outside of sales situations, to really understand what drives their decisions every day.*"
> — *Verena Liedgens, Agruppa (Colombia)*

# Brand promises: give your word.

The final step in value propositions is giving each audience and every persona a small set of the most persuasive reasons the personas should notice you and take the action you're asking for.

Think of these as your promise of value to be delivered to your audience. What do you help them accomplish functionally? How do you make their lives better and richer emotionally, as well?

### CLIENT EXAMPLE: BASMEH & ZEITOONEH
بسمة وزيتونة

- *Institutional funder Isaac: "Gaps in aid exist and refugee-led organizations like ours — with history and credibility — help you reach the full scope of your agenda."*

- *Philanthropic foundation Frannie: "Communities are best positioned to make lasting change, and we have a history of impact."*

- *High-net-worth Henry: "While the region as a whole is unstable, you can trust the team you're investing in."*

---

For this client working in Syria and Lebanon, we first took their three donor audiences. We gave each a fictional name and persona. Then we thought about Basmeh & Zeitooneh's three uniques: refugee-led, embedded in community, and history/credibility. For each of those audiences and each unique, we simply crafted a series of statements that would reflect the type of brand promise our client could communicate in their fundraising.

## ACTION STEP: CRAFT YOUR PROMISES

Go back to your audiences and consider the empathy map you just produced for each. Then make a list of all the features, advantages, and benefits they'll get by supporting your organization.

- You're trying to answer the question your audience will constantly ask when considering whether or not to engage with you: "What's in this for me?"

- How do you make their lives easier or better? Repeat this process for each of the three audiences. Then weave these brand promises into compelling messaging.

Brand promises can be functional, emotional, or social. The higher up the ladder, the more powerful it becomes. Because: features *tell*, advantages *compel*, benefits *sell*.

So your fundraising should communicate all three. Here's the breakdown:

**Features:** What you do and how the product or program works.

**Advantages:** How the features help your customers or community.

**Benefits:** The outcomes or changes in conditions that result.

*"Features vs. advantages vs. benefits = what the product is vs. what the product does vs. how the product makes you feel." — Harry Dry, marketing thought leader (England)*

Since many nonprofit leaders struggle to communicate their model simply, features are important to explain first. But don't stop there. Because changes in conditions always beat the number of people reached. That's why advantages and benefits are the most powerful value propositions.

Especially for donors.

This art of messaging at all three levels — called *brand laddering* — can be game-changing for your communications.

Just as Coca-Cola doesn't tell you about its fizzy, colored fructose syrup. They sell you *a Coke and a smile*. Dove soap doesn't discuss vegetable oil and animal fat in its campaigns. It communicates body positivity and *real beauty* to women. Toyota promises reliability and peace of mind.

And on and on.

Yes, value proposition laddering works for nonprofit brands, too. Take, for instance, a fictional eye-health social enterprise:

**Feature:** Free eyeglasses for kids.

**Advantage:** Students with improved sight.

**Benefit:** Increased learning outcomes in school.

So, what level of value proposition are you communicating? Don't just inform. Inspire action.

One of the best ways to inspire that action is to combine your value propositions with a compelling brand personality, coming up next in Chapter 9.

Because boring brands make funders yawn.

# Summary.

1. The value propositions section of your positioning strategy includes uniques, audiences, personas, and promises.

2. Funders (and all human brains) are wired for comparison, so determining — and saying! — how you're unique is an important part of fundraising.

3. No nonprofit can afford to communicate with everyone, so you must pick your top three audiences at which you'll aim your upcoming marketing communications.

4. Naming your audiences isn't enough — you must truly understand their pains and gains by developing an empathy map.

5. With empathy in mind, you can create a set of brand promises that ladder up from features to advantages and ultimately to benefits.

# 9. BRAND PERSONALITY

## Clear brands attract. Compelling brands convert.

There's an organization I just have to tell you about: FRIDA (The Young Feminist Fund). And I want to see if I can describe its brand personality in words only, no visuals.

The name, FRIDA, tells you plenty as an acronym for Flexibility, Resources, Inclusivity, Diversity, and Action — with a nod to the famous Mexican painter Frida Kahlo. FRIDA is the only fund run by young feminists for other emerging feminist organizations, collectives, and movements.

Instead of a basic theory of change, they publish a beautiful *Garden of Change* — a hand-drawn, brightly colored illustration of their problem statement, solution, outcomes, and vision, mixed in among plants, rivers, and desert landscapes.

They have unflinching messaging — like "storms of solidarity" and "we can spark beautiful beginnings, magical moments, and feminist futures." Plus they have created a brave visual identity — progressive typography, colorful illustrations, a quirky logo, and a grantee map flipped upside down so that, for once, the Global South sits on top.

And here's a quick story to illustrate how radical their brand is:

*"FRIDA receives about 1,000 applicants per grantmaking cycle, who are then invited to comment and vote on the 100 groups that they think should receive funding. One group applied, received one of the highest ratings from their peers, but then stepped back and offered their FRIDA grant to another group that they felt needed the money more." — Edgar Villanueva, author and decolonizing wealth activist (Lumbee Tribe of North Carolina)*

Now you tell me: doesn't FRIDA sound like an intriguing brand? And if you check out their website or social media, are the visuals anything like the personality you pictured?

FRIDA illustrates why it's never enough to have clear communications. You must also be *compelling*. And compelling means more than bold colors (like FRIDA also has), which we'll cover in the visual identity chapter later on. Because there are millions of nonprofits in the world, all vying for the same fundraising attention.

The best way to make your brand stand out? A bold brand personality. The good news is that it's not too difficult to determine a brand personality and then to embody it in every element of your communications: from visuals to writing to websites.

Brand function gets you noticed, but brand personality seals the deal. It's not just about what you offer but what your brand says to people. When they think, *this feels right*, that's your brand's true power. It's the most valuable thing you own.

You can think of a brand personality like the personality of a human. Each of us has an inner core: ambition, beliefs, values, and so on. And we each have a personality, which affects how we present ourselves to others in the way we dress, walk, and talk.

The traits you choose to highlight in your brand will shape its personality and perception. Without a clear definition, your brand risks coming off as inconsistent or confusing. So pin down your brand's personality, or it will define itself — often not in the way you want.

It's best to decide now. *Who* do you want your brand to be?

In this brand personality chapter, you'll learn how to determine your **brand character, traits,** and **tradition.**

## Brand character: show yourself.

Humans are wired for stories. They give us the context for forces too big to grasp. In a few seconds, a story can cut through the noise and make your message hit home. Use what people already know to make them feel something new.

Psychologist Carl Jung[1] believed story characters are instantly familiar to us because they are primal and instinctive — what he termed a "collective unconscious" that we all share. The character (or archetype) is a deep reflection of a brand's personality.

There are 12 archetypes that Jung identified and then named, which brand builders started applying to organizations. These characters range from those that convey comfort to others that create excitement. Choosing the right archetype is essential. Brands that capture meaning and communicate that message in subtle and refined ways dominate the field.

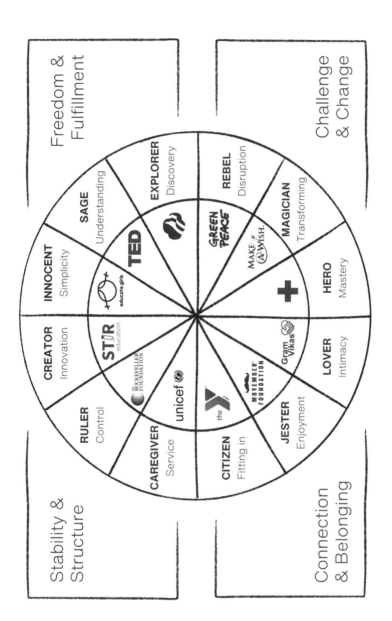

FIGURE 16: Brand character wheel.

**ACTION STEP: PICK A BRAND CHARACTER (OR TWO)**

Conduct a full brand personality exercise to establish your special characteristics.

- Go to one of the many free online quizzes, such as brandpersonalityquiz.com.

- Have your entire leadership team complete the quiz, and debate your results.

- Search online to read more about the character or two that feels right — there are many great resources out there.

- Then determine a powerful brand character/ archetype, then lean into it for all internal and external communications.

# Traits: think, feel, speak, behave.

Your brand's traits will inform both visual and verbal communications, from marketing materials to your employee handbook to speeches and images. They should infuse every aspect of your brand.

Your traits and voice are all about establishing how you deliver your message.

*"People don't always remember what you say or even what you do, but they always remember how you made them feel."* — *Maya Angelou, poet and civil rights activist (United States)*

For our clients, we simply list a few traits that their brand should *always* and *never* embody. This becomes an easy, short-hand tool for future marketing communications and fundraising.

## CLIENT EXAMPLES

*Vega Coffee*

- **Always**: Charismatic, empathetic, bold, informed.

- **Never**: Arrogant, aggressive, pretentious, boring.

*Ubuntu Life*

- **Always**: Proudly Kenyan, warm, inspiring, playful.

- **Never**: Serious, pitying, divisive, degrading.

*Blood:Water*

- **Always**: Sincere, multifaceted, trusted, respectful, curious.

- **Never**: Ordinary, exclusive, traditional, quiet.

**ACTION STEP: FIND YOUR TRAITS**

Think back to the brand character you picked.

- List five words/traits that your brand will always embody.

- List five words/traits that your brand will never embody.

- These traits should apply to all your messaging and communications.

# Tradition: patterns, practices, and principles.

Traditions are organizational customs that develop organically. They naturally build your culture and can be a powerful tool for maintaining it as you grow your funding.

And traditions can be subtle internal reinforcements of your external brand personality and positioning.

## CLIENT EXAMPLES

*Reach for Change: Make time for fika!*

*JUST: Three deep breaths and one word.*

---

Our client Reach for Change was Swedish, where "fika" (an afternoon snack) is a big tradition. They brought this practice to their work worldwide and donors even knew it about their brand — but this exercise made it formal. Our client JUST begins every meeting with everyone taking three breaths, then sharing a one-word feeling. They do this even with funders on a conference call, reinforcing this brand tradition.

## ACTION STEP: NAME YOUR TRADITION

You can't be overly prescriptive or force a tradition. There's also no formula for right or wrong traditions.

- A tradition has to be authentic.

- Think of activities, behaviors, or mantras.

- If one doesn't exist, just keep your eyes open. One may come to you!

Now you hopefully see why I say, boring brands make funders yawn. Then guess what? You did it — the positioning strategy section is wrapped.

You're about to move into marketing communications, a set of practices that amplify your story and convert audiences into supporters.

And the second half of being findable.

# Summary.

1. The brand personality section of your positioning strategy includes character, traits, style, and tradition.

2. It's never enough to have clear communications. You must also be compelling.

3. Your brand character — one of 12 archetypes you can choose — is a powerful way to develop a compelling brand that stands out.

4. Stemming from that character choice, you must determine five traits your brand will always (and never) embody.

5. Traditions are internal customs or practices that can often reflect on your personality as seen by the outside world.

# MARKETING COMMUNICATIONS

Amplify your story and mobilize funder audiences with these promotional practices.

Whistling can travel up to 5,000 meters[1] — more than 10 times the distance of shouting.[2]

A whistle's energy is focused in a single high-pitched note. So, it's easily distinguished from background noise. That's why, long before phones were invented, whistle languages developed in mountainous or heavily forested communities around the world. In fact, *Smithsonian Magazine* says that more than 80 cultures (from Bolivia to Burma) still use a whistled form of their native language for long-distance conversations.

This fun fact is a lesson for all nonprofits: we don't have to yell in our marketing communications. But we *do* have to at least whistle.

Hard work, intelligent products and programs, and extraordinary impact happen daily in the social sector. Yet much of it goes unseen and unheard. You don't have to focus on marketing communications to achieve social change. But it's almost impossible to reach significant funding without it.

It's the second piece of becoming findable.

My Founding Partner Kathleen Souder asks this critical question:

*"What would climate change advocacy look like without Greta Thunberg's appearances on late-night TV? Racial justice without the social media takeover of Black Lives Matter? Global health without Paul Farmer's Mountains Beyond Mountains?"*

We cheer for nonprofits that prioritize marketing and communications, breaking away from a sector that often lags behind. But too many leaders still see marcom as a sideline — a distraction rather than a driving force of impact.

Marketing can feel like chaos. No set rules, no clear path, just endless ways to shout your brand's name. But you can't do it all. So where *do* you put your focus?

In this section, you'll learn more about marketing communications: **what it is, why it matters,** and **how to create your marcom.** Then you'll fully work on the main parts of marketing communications in Chapters 10–16.

# What it is.

Marketing communications is a broad term for a broad category. It includes branding, storytelling, mass-market advertising, direct marketing, PR, digital media, promotion, sponsorships, events, and more.

My definition? Marcom is saying the right things to the right people in the right places at the right time to drive the right results.

Marcom is the use of various channels and tools to communicate a message to a desired market. It's all the ways by which a nonprofit can educate and urge audiences — directly or indirectly — about its products and programs.

> *"The practical reality is that both words, marketing and communications, are used interchangeably in the nonprofit sector. Marketing is about the value exchange. Communications, on the other hand, is all of the content you create and your plan to distribute that content so that you can maintain relationships with the people consuming that content. Every nonprofit needs both."* — Kivi Leroux Miller, nonprofit marketing author (United States)

Depending on your model, communications can be more about general awareness and reputation building. Whereas marketing is often focused on generating leads for your product or service (or even donations). Both of which can increase fundraising, but not always immediately.

> *"I have found it very useful for non-comms people to separate communication from marketing and sales or fundraising. That makes it easier to set reasonable expectations. I remember being frustrated because the phone didn't ring after the first time we were mentioned in the newspaper. It was a communication success, not a fundraising failure."* — Leonardo Letelier, Sitawi (Brazil)

# Why it matters: communications is your mission too.

Like it or not, nonprofit leaders: you're not only in the business of fighting poverty and injustice. You're also in the business of developing and advancing big, bold ideas.

A research project called Communication Matters[3] in the *Stanford Social Innovation Review* found that nonprofits excelling at communications are stronger, smarter, and vastly more effective. The author, Sean Gibbons, notes that communications is no longer an appendage to the work, but an integral part. "Strategic communications can revolutionize your organization and exponentially expand your impact," he says. In other words, all of the advice in this book won't pull you away from "the real work" — this *is* the work, too.

> *"Halting climate change. Eradicating disease. Lifting up the arts. Ending poverty. At their core, foundations and nonprofits are in the business of developing and advancing big, bold ideas. If you want your ideas to take hold and win, you need to communicate and communicate well."* — Sean Gibbons, nonprofit communications advocate (United States)

A grantmaker in that research project echoed the same importance: "Tell me one major, successful social change initiative that did not have very strong communications as part of its success."

Yet our society continues to give nonprofits a different set of rules than corporate brands. And this discrimination has warped our sector. We think that advertising and marketing are no-no's, according to a TED Talk from Dan Pallotta, titled *The way we think about charity is dead wrong.*[4]

We must rethink this myth — the so-called radical notion of spending donor dollars on communications.

"I don't want my donation spent on advertising, I want it to go to the needy," claims the average naive donor. But money invested in advertising could bring in dramatically more money for the needy, says Pallotta. It's simple math. And simple logic.

> *"Brilliant experts can write compelling policy papers filled with breakthrough ideas to make our society better. But they can't influence and shape the debate if no one is reading and digesting their work. That means organizations must invest in communications. And if you look at the most successful organizations — no matter their mission — you'll see that a strong and fully integrated communications strategy is always an important part of what they do." — Daniella Leger, nonprofit communications leader (United States)*

The power of marcom has been proven — over and over again — in the private sector. There are many examples that nonprofits can learn from. Because, at the end of the day, social sector organizations are businesses, too (like I said in the introduction). *Forbes* found that communicating consistently across platforms increases revenue by 23%. Aberdeen Strategy & Research says companies with strong marcom achieve 20% annual growth.[6]

So it should be obvious. Improving your brand communications impacts the bottom line significantly. From increased donor conversions, to landing more foundation grants and impact investment, to driving greater sales.

Yet marketing communications isn't merely about driving income. You've heard me beat the drum that a strong brand and good marcom can generate impact, too. Whether they be the less-tangible values of reaching beneficiaries, influencing government partners, or recruiting staff and volunteers.

So communications isn't secondary. It's a primary force.

Comms isn't a line item. It's your lifeline.

## How to create your marketing communications.

First things first. Everyone wants better marketing communications, but marketing communications never begins with marketing communications. Instead, it begins with a solid theory of change and positioning strategy.

As I said above, marketing communications isn't one single thing. It's a collection of work. And at Mighty Ally, our marcom work is the meatiest of anything we do (and thus, the meatiest part of this book).

Here's the high-level summary of how to build your marcom engine:

**Marketing plan:** In Chapter 10 you'll determine your aims, tactics, and resources.

**Messaging & storytelling:** Then in Chapter 11, you will learn seven tools to clarify your story.

**Writing & thought leadership:** After you establish that core messaging, in Chapter 12 you can focus on how to write and spread your thoughts.

**Visual identity:** How you look matters for what you say, so in Chapter 13 you'll learn about designing the visual side of your brand (meaning, brand-*ing*).

**Pitch deck:** In Chapter 14, you'll unpack a five-section formula to start productive conversations with funders.

**Website strategy:** In Chapter 15, you will translate your brand strategy into the most important marcom touchpoint.

**Corporate partnerships:** And we'll end this section with Chapter 16, where you'll learn how to amplify your brand via CSR, or corporate social responsibility.

This big discipline of marcom is way too much to fit into a neat one-page blueprint. But we can at least distill down the most essential information, as shown in Figure 17.

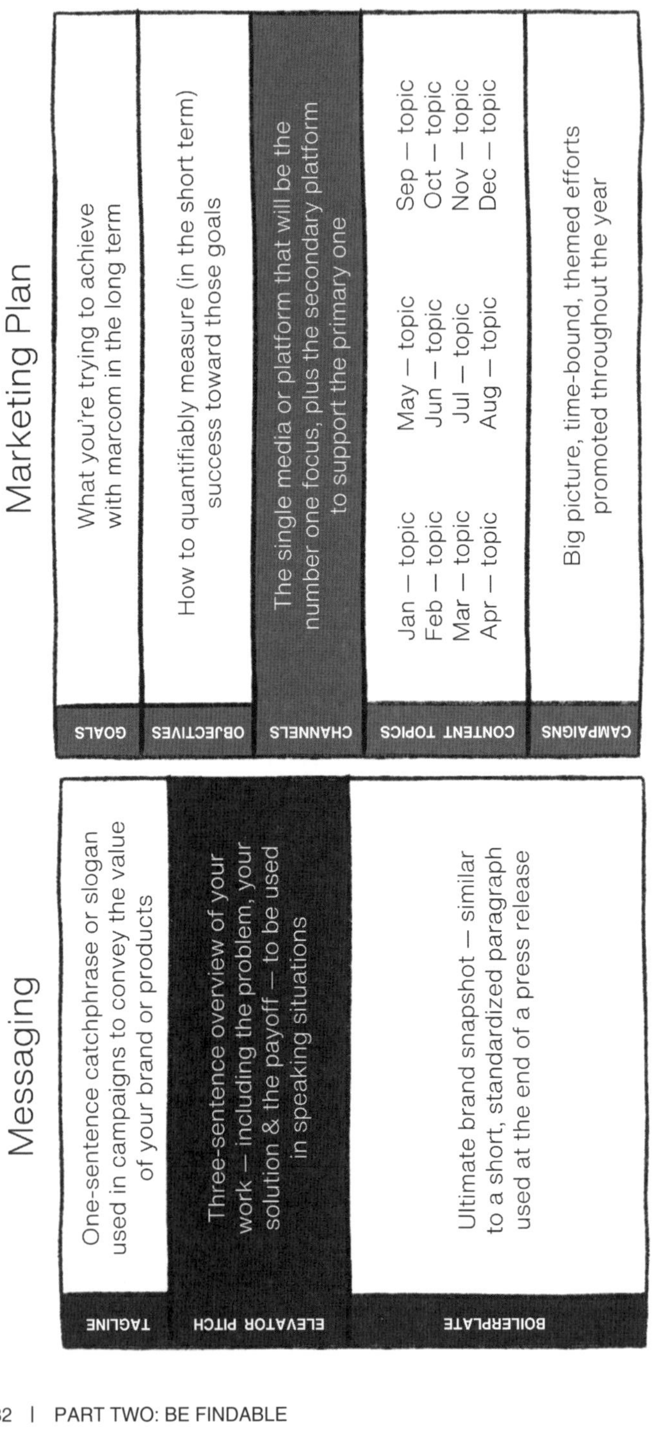

## Marketing Plan

**GOALS** — What you're trying to achieve with marcom in the long term

**OBJECTIVES** — How to quantifiably measure (in the short term) success toward those goals

**CHANNELS** — The single media or platform that will be the number one focus, plus the secondary platform to support the primary one

**CONTENT TOPICS** —
Jan — topic
Feb — topic
Mar — topic
Apr — topic
May — topic
Jun — topic
Jul — topic
Aug — topic
Sep — topic
Oct — topic
Nov — topic
Dec — topic

**CAMPAIGNS** — Big picture, time-bound, themed efforts promoted throughout the year

## Messaging

**TAGLINE** — One-sentence catchphrase or slogan used in campaigns to convey the value of your brand or products

**ELEVATOR PITCH** — Three-sentence overview of your work — including the problem, your solution & the payoff — to be used in speaking situations

**BOILERPLATE** — Ultimate brand snapshot — similar to a short, standardized paragraph used at the end of a press release

FIGURE 17: The Mighty Ally marketing communications blueprint.

It's worth noting that each of the marketing communications chapters (10–16) is a relatively light touch. Because there's a plethora of resources available, even entire books written, about all of these topics. From messaging to visuals.

My goal is for you to have a basic understanding of each marcom building block, know how they relate to each other and how they help fix your fundraising, and see that most people overcomplicate these topics.

You can do this. We *have to* do this. Despite the tireless work of millions of people worldwide to improve our collective quality of life, our sector has a long way to go.

We can't claim that committing to marcom will help us solve poverty and injustice. But we *do* know that without a commitment to amplify the brands of those making an impact, we'll never get there.

So get to it. Tell your story. Share your expertise. Connect with donors. Raise awareness. Do this with confidence, knowing that the effort isn't a distraction from or an addendum to your work. It's part of the work itself.

*"Marketing takes a day to learn. Unfortunately, it takes a lifetime to master." — Philip Kotler, business consultant (United States)*

## The minimalist communications playbook.

If you take away nothing else from the marcom section of this book, just make sure you have a:

- 10-slide deck

- Five-page website

- Three-line elevator pitch

- Monthly email newsletter

You can do all four for cheap, or even for free. And, combined, they can raise millions in fundraising.

Let's be honest. Your comms team is small. Stretched thin. Maybe even nonexistent. You, as the leader, might even be handling marcom on your own. So until those four primary marketing assets are 100% optimized, ignore everything else.

No social media. No direct mail. No speeches. No podcasts. No events. No video. No ads. No PR. Not until you do the basic stuff well.

Because brands that simplify first, amplify most. Brands that focus on fundamentals, find the funds. And those fundamentals begin in your marketing plan, up next in Chapter 10.

# Summary.

1. A good marketing communications mix includes a marketing plan, messaging and storytelling, writing and thought leadership, visual identity, pitch deck, website strategy, and corporate CSR partnerships.

2. Marketing communications is a big bucket with no shared definition. But it's really just saying the right things to the right people in the right places at the right time to drive the right results.

3. No matter your nonprofit's mission, communications is your work, too. It is your mission, as well. As Sean Gibbons reminds us, "At their core, foundations and nonprofits are in the business of developing and advancing big, bold ideas."

4. You can think of at least three distinct reasons for developing your marcom: general/reputational communications, marketing/sales, and fundraising.

5. At the very least, you should develop the minimal communications playbook: a 10-slide deck, a five-page website, a three-line elevator pitch, and a monthly email newsletter.

# 10. MARKETING PLAN

## Brands that chase all channels chase away funding.

"We need to start posting on Instagram, right?"

"I think we should be sending out more emails each month."

"That nonprofit always has great direct mail, and we have none!"

We hear statements like these all the time. Clients come to us, feeling inundated by all the channels available to them — unsure of where and how to start.

Here's some good news: you don't have to do it all. In fact, you shouldn't. But you *can* experiment.

> "Take a risk and keep testing; what works today won't
> work tomorrow, but what worked yesterday may work
> again." — Amrita Sahasrabudhe, consultant (United States)

A good marcom plan is made up of the following three parts, which you'll learn about in this chapter: **aims** (goals and objectives); **tactics** (channels, content topics, content types, and campaigns); and **resources** (timeline and budget).

# Goals: what are you aiming for?

First up, determine how marketing communications will help you maximize funding or advance social justice. In other words, what are you trying to accomplish with your marcom?

You will have many other goals for your organization — but here we're only thinking about those goals for which comms can be responsible.

---

**CLIENT EXAMPLE: JUSTICE DEFENDERS**

- *Amplify stories and content from people in prisons.*

- *Generate additional unrestricted, long-term funding.*

- *Raise brand awareness — both internationally and locally.*

---

When we worked with Justice Defenders, we had to raise awareness. We wanted to tell more stories from people with lived experience, to capitalize on this unique differentiator in their positioning strategy. And finally, they needed to move beyond smaller, restricted institutional grants — the main goal out of all of these.

**ACTION STEP: DETERMINE YOUR MARCOM GOALS**

- Choose 2–3 goals that will last an entire year. Achieving more than that is not realistic, given your limited resources.

- These are big-picture, long-term aims. Not the exact short-term numbers or targets you're trying to reach (we'll define those next, as objectives).

- Keep them simple and concrete. Describe each goal in a single sentence.

# Objectives: how to measure those goals.

Drilling down from your big-picture marketing communications goals, let's get a bit more granular. We need to know the exact measures you're trying to meet. That way, we can determine the right channels, content, and campaigns.

Whereas goals are long-term and less tangible, your objectives are shorter-term and highly measurable.

## CLIENT EXAMPLE: JUSTICE DEFENDERS

- *Online donations received.*

- *New high-net-worth club members.*

- *Amount of institutional funding generated.*

- *Number of donors in the monthly community.*

Same client example as the goals above. Now, you can see from these objectives that this client was focused, focused, focused on funding. Primarily, we wanted to drive new online donations and sign-ups for its monthly giving clubs.

## ACTION STEP: DRAFT YOUR OBJECTIVES

- Use benchmark data from past efforts if you have it. Or start with general targets and get precise as you go.

- Set 3–5 objectives that are necessary to reach your goals. Then make sure they are SMARTIE: specific, measurable, attainable, realistic, timebound, inclusive, and equitable.

- Keep in mind that individual channels or campaigns (up next) could have even-more-specific objectives. But these are the measures for the overall plan.

# Channels: countless tactics to choose.

It's helpful to think of marcom in four buckets: paid, earned, shared, and owned (PESO).[1]

Paid media is just what it sounds like — it costs money — such as Google Ads or billboards. Earned media is primarily out of your control but still free, such as word of mouth or publicity mentions. Shared media mostly consists of social media (stay tuned: you don't *own* your followers!). And owned media is everything you control directly, like your blog posts and email database.

FIGURE 18: The PESO mix — paid, earned, shared, owned.

Only big NGOs and private sector brands can pull off this PESO model all at once. Because there are advantages and disadvantages of each category.

**Paid media:** It's scalable, reliable, and fast, but it's also expensive, it's low trust, and returns stop when you stop investing.

**Earned media:** It's authoritative, cost-effective, and long-term but also unreliable, hard to scale, and expensive.

**Shared media:** It's highly trusted and has low cost but is also unreliable and unscalable.

**Owned media:** It's low-risk and long-term but slow — requiring paid, earned, or shared media to build.

For early- and growth-stage brands, we recommend selecting just two channels: pick a primary channel, then choose a secondary channel to augment the primary. Nonprofits almost always have small marcom teams and budgets. You have to focus, but of course be flexible enough if special opportunities arise.

> *"You are everywhere, but you don't have to be. Strategy is a decision to take a path, to say no." — Kristina Halvorson, content strategist (United States)*

## CLIENT EXAMPLES

*Peek Vision*

- *Primary: Email newsletter*

- *Secondary: LinkedIn*

*JUST*

- *Primary: Facebook*

- *Secondary: Email marketing*

*Coalition for Good Schools*

- *Primary: Member amplification*

- *Secondary: Convening events*

---

Two of these three clients had email marketing as a top two channel. Coalition for Good Schools was a start-up when we worked with them, and they didn't yet have an email database. But they did have a coalition of supportive members with their own email lists that they could tap into.

## ACTION STEP: CHOOSE YOUR PRIORITY CHANNELS

- Think about your priority audiences (back to positioning strategy). Where can you best reach them — both online and offline?

- Pick a primary channel. And choose a secondary channel to augment the first.

- Your website — with some sort of active content — is your brand hub, not one of these two channels.

- Everything else is considered tertiary.

- Keep track of data and adjust accordingly.

## Donor inboxes are the gateway to giving.

Before you pick your channels, it's worth a reminder: email marketing drives $36 for every $1 spent.[2] Higher than any other comms channel.

> *"Paid ads may seem like the easy way to get your organization noticed, but 'easy' is not always affordable."*
> *— Nicole Giuffra, content marketer (Italy)*

There's a reason the greatest, biggest brands in the world still send regular, purposeful email newsletters. Because they're focused on results, not vanity.

You own your email list.

You rent your social following.

A best-selling author once said he wouldn't trade his two million email subscribers for 100 million Instagram followers. That's telling.

Because as long as you keep a copy of your email subscribers locally, those addresses are yours forever. But no matter what you do or how many social followers you amass, they could vanish overnight.

TikTok was almost banned. Instagram can delete your account. LinkedIn could go under.

Not to mention, nearly everyone receives your message when you email your subscribers. On social media, less than 10% of your followers will see your post.

Plus, most links shared on social media are never clicked on. Because the algorithm prioritizes *zero-click content* to keep users from leaving the platform. So if you're promoting a new blog post, a media article, or a donation page, a limited social audience likely won't click, anyway.

But people *do* click emails. And there are 4.3 billion daily email users globally. That's more than half of humanity, still growing rapidly, and roughly the same number as social users worldwide.

The takeaway: do both.

Just like I do: posting on LinkedIn helps drive subscribers to my Substack newsletter.

But nonprofits should spend three to four times the effort on email marketing than on social media. Year after year, email remains that valuable. Inbox impact beats social scrolls.

## Content topics: you need themes for those channels.

Got your channels lined up? Great. Now think: how will you grab attention and make people stop scrolling?

There's no one-size-fits-all. Some organizations use their uniques to develop content topics. Others hammer home what they do — their interventions. These evergreen content topics can run throughout the year and supplement more timely topics, like monthly themes.

Aim to have 5–12 topic areas that will guide anyone drafting your content. That way, if you have five total, you can use one topic each day of the week (like on social media). Or, if you pick 12 topics, you can use one topic each month of the year.

Again, mix and match. There's no perfect formula.

## CLIENT EXAMPLES

*Community Health Impact Coalition*

- *Monday: General proCHW content*
- *Tuesday: Members, allies, and CHWs*
- *Wednesday: CHIC tools and resources*
- *Thursday: CHIC events and campaigns*
- *Friday: CHIC work and wins*

*Nyaka*

- *January: Film screening*
- *February: Women's Day*
- *March: Grannies program*
- *April: Mother's Day*
- *May: Education*
- *June: Sponsor a student*
- *July: Sexual & gender-based violence walk*
- *August: Health/nutrition*
- *September: Galas and events*
- *October: NYC Marathon*
- *November: Giving Tuesday*
- *December: Holiday giving*

---

The first client here, CHIC, decided to pick a different topic for a different day of the week — communications was a big part of their work, so that felt right. The second client, Nyaka, didn't want to change topics daily, so they chose 12 topics (one for each month in the year).

**ACTION STEP: BRAINSTORM CONTENT TOPICS**

- Refer back to your goals.

- Then think about topics that could make your audiences take notice.

- What content do you have now? Or what topics would you like to develop?

- For example, pick five daily topics, e.g., Women's Wednesdays.

- Or, pick 12 monthly topics, e.g., Mother's Day May.

# Content types: which forms of media will you use?

Next, we need to determine the types of content you'll develop around those content topics you just named. These *types* are the actual forms of media you'll produce.

There's a plethora of content types you could use. We don't have to get stuck thinking that social media means just photos and text. Or that website content is only about blogging.

Instead, let's explore what's possible in Figure 19.

# Content Types

| | | |
|---|---|---|
| Blogs & vlogs | Organizational news | Competitions |
| Photos | Tools | Promotions |
| Videos | Quizzes | Webinars |
| Text posts | Survey reports | Infographics |
| Listicles | Notion swipe files | eBooks |
| Threads | Q&As | Audiobooks |
| Carousels | FAQs | Book reviews |
| Case studies | How-to guides | Memes |
| Research/white papers | Templates | Animated GIFs |
| Presentation slides | Community content | Event summaries |
| Online courses | Interviews | Checklists |
| Guest posts | Press releases | Polls |
| Livestreams | Downloads | Annual reports |
| Roundups | Testimonials | Impact reports |
| Sector news | Wikis | Virtual tours |

FIGURE 19: Content type options for your marketing communications.

You might be surprised by how much brand content already exists — which you can readily repurpose — while conducting your everyday business.

For example, take one M&E report and create a case study for donors, a webinar for NGO partners, a virtual tour for website visitors, a how-to-guide for other nonprofits, a presentation slides deck for media, a press release for government officials or a series of testimonials for the community.

*"Some of the best content is going unseen because the team behind it hasn't embraced distribution. It's never reshared. It's not amplified by the team. It's never promoted in a community. And it's only promoted for a week. Create once. Distribute forever."* — Ross Simmonds, distribution speaker and author (Canada)[3]

---

**ACTION STEP: THINK OF YOUR CONTENT TYPES**

- Pick a mix of 4–5 main content types you'll use and reuse often.

- Which types do your audiences consume/prefer?

- Where are your strengths and interests internally? Do you like writing? Is there a great photographer on staff?

- Sprinkle in some alternative types. Remember, some types perform better on certain channels.

- But resist the urge to do it all. You can't and shouldn't.

---

## Campaigns: big distinct rallying points.

In addition to the content topics you brainstormed, you should create 2–3 distinct campaigns to run throughout the year. A campaign is a planned communications series designed to generate excitement, participation, or donations around a single theme. And support your marcom goals. Launch one when you need a unified message to engage your audience and reach a specific milestone.

You can get really creative here. And if you focus on just 2–3 campaigns per year, you can take more time to plan and implement.

> *"You can't buy engagement, you have to build engagement." — Tara-Nicholle Kirke, author (Portugal)*

## CLIENT EXAMPLES

*Nyaka*

- *Mother's Day*
- *Giving Tuesday*
- *Documentary launch*

*Vega Coffee*

- *Get woke up.*
- *Rise. Shine. Disrupt.*
- *Fuel the resistance.*

---

Some campaigns can be more straightforward, like Nyaka's choosing two big giving days plus a documentary film they were launching. Other campaigns can be more creative and conceptual, as with Vega Coffee.

**ACTION STEP: OUTLINE A FEW CAMPAIGN IDEAS**

- What are your big moments throughout the year?

- What old piece of content could you repurpose and republish?

- Does any of this new brand strategy need extra announcements?

- Do you have any of these big moments or documents coming up?

- Are there any prominent international days you could rally around?

# Resources: timeline and budget.

You've made it this far. Your marcom aims and tactics are set. All that's left is assigning the right resources — a timeline and a budget to pull off the plan.

The Chinese philosopher Lao Tzu famously remarked, "To say I don't have time is like saying I don't want to." So let's be clear about when this work will get done.

And, as for budget, remember that free can only take you so far. Sure, there are plenty of ways to amplify your brand for free. Beyond that, you'll have to pay in order to level up your brand.

*"If you think your organization needs a bigger marketing budget, maybe you just need to be less average instead."* — Seth Godin, best-selling marketing author (United States)

That quote is harsh, but true.

And it's exactly why we did all your theory of change, strategic planning, and positioning work *before* marketing communications. To make you anything but average.

Now it's time to tell your donors how extraordinary you are, in actual words.

And that's what Chapter 11 is all about: messaging and storytelling, helping you give donors a story to remember, not a fact to memorize.

# Summary.

1. The marcom plan section of your marketing communications includes your aims, tactics, and resources.

2. Goals are big-picture, long-term, broad statements you can accomplish through 3–5 objectives (short/mid-term, detailed, and measurable).

3. The PESO model will help you pick your channels, but always prioritize owned assets like email marketing over shared channels like social media.

4. If you develop content topics and content types in advance, it will make your day-to-day marketing communications easier — and more effective.

5. As Ross Simmonds advises, "create once, distribute forever." This philosophy ensures that your hard work isn't lost when only a few people see your initial efforts.

# 11. MESSAGING & STORYTELLING
## Give donors a story to remember, not a fact to memorize.

Bryan Stevenson earned the lengthiest standing ovation in TED Talks history. As the nonprofit founder of Equal Justice Initiative, he spoke about a challenging, complex topic: America's criminal justice system. And he raised $1 million in donations that night from a single speech.

How?

He told stories for 65% of his presentation.[1] About his grandmother, about Rosa Parks, about not drinking beer as a kid. In fact, he spoke for five minutes straight before introducing a single statistic about U.S. prisons.

> *"You need data, facts, and analysis to challenge people, but you also need narrative to get people comfortable enough to care about the community that you are advocating for. Your audience needs to be willing to go with you on a journey."* — *Bryan Stevenson, nonprofit leader (United States)*

That's why you don't need more numbers in your fundraising. Instead, go get:

- Quotes
- Interviews
- Illustrations
- Testimonials
- Event recaps
- Photo essays
- Success stories
- Staff reflections
- Before-and-afters
- Partner shoutouts
- Historical context
- Community voices
- Volunteer experiences
- Stakeholder perspectives

People aren't calculators. They're storytellers. Think about the last nonprofit that caught your attention. Do you remember its impact data? Or was it their storytelling that made you take notice?

> *"In recent years, advances in neuroscience have helped us to understand that the brain processes meaning before detail." — For Impact, fundraising firm (global)*

Mighty Ally runs a three-year training program for the Dovetail Impact Foundation portfolio. Dovetail is a donor that's really big on results. Heck, *impact* is in their name. But we spend the entire first year guiding these early-stage organizations to get their theory of change, positioning strategy, communications, and pitch deck in order. Their brand. Only in the second year does Dovetail bring in monitoring, evaluation, and data experts.

Don't get me wrong.

Investing in measurement is simply the right thing to do for impact accountability. So narrative plus numbers is the ultimate fundraising combination. But, as I think back to all the years of hearing our funder clients talk about a nonprofit brand, they never lead with a data point.

It's always a sticky anecdote.

Numbers tell.

Stories sell.

> *"People would rather believe than know."* — E. O. Wilson, biologist (United States)

In this chapter, you'll learn **why storytelling matters, what messaging and storytelling is,** and **how to create a messaging and storytelling platform.**

# Why storytelling matters: good stories beat good spreadsheets.

Donors don't act because of your data. They initially fund their beliefs about you (based on emotional signals), then justify that gift with logic.

Even if they don't admit it.

*Harvard Business Review* found that 95% of our purchase decisions occur unconsciously.[2] And that our conscious mind will later even make up reasons to validate our unconscious choices.

> *"Stories are persuasive, data is just proof. Once the donor is persuaded, however, you may need to reinforce their decision-making with a little proof."* — Claire Axelrad, J.D., CFRE, *fundraising coach (United States)*

In other words, your spreadsheets or metrics alone don't attract or secure the funding. Those figures only help determine the amount you receive.

"People forget facts, but they never forget a good story," Axelrad reminds us. That's why data wrapped in a story is 22 times more memorable.[3]

Here's more. 56% of social media users who donate online said compelling storytelling makes them give the most, according to Nonprofit Tech for Good.[4] Stories were the number one motivation, while data wasn't even on the list.

So whether we're fighting the powers of corruption or the unjust imbalances in philanthropy, words matter:

*"Until the lion learns how to write, every story will glorify the hunter." — African proverb*

# What messaging is.

Your messaging and storytelling platform does for words what your visual guide does for design. It's the backbone of your brand's voice. And packed with ready-to-use content, key phrases, and strategic copy blocks. Whenever you need to write a pitch, a newsletter, or a website update, this is your starting point to ensure that every message hits home.

A successful messaging and storytelling platform will serve your future marketing communications endeavors by:

- Minimizing the chances of going off-brand when scrambling to meet a tight deadline.

- Maximizing communication efficiencies without reinventing the wheel each time.

- Making it easier to outsource copywriting for comms materials.

- Strengthening brand equity and consistency over time.

- Creating internal clarity, confidence, and alignment.

# How to create your messaging and storytelling platform.

Your messaging and storytelling platform should contain the following elements, which you'll learn how to create below: **tagline, elevator pitch, message map, public narrative,** and **boilerplate.**

## Tagline.

Your organization's tagline is a descriptor, catchphrase, or motto which is often seen coupled with your name or logo. It's a powerful punch that tells people exactly who you are and what you stand for. Whether it's practical or inspiring, your tagline should stick in the mind, making people remember your organization long after encountering your brand. Think of it as a quick trigger for the value you offer — whenever donors hear it, they think of you.

**CLIENT EXAMPLES**

*Nyaka: For our children's sake.*

*Oxfam: The future is equal.*

*Coalition for Good Schools: Preventing violence against children, one good school at a time.*

---

Two of these taglines are short and sweet, the other more literal. There's no perfect formula.

## ACTION STEP: DEVELOP A TAGLINE

- No more than 10 words.

- It can sometimes be similar to your 8-word mission statement, your reason for being, or your vision. So that's an excellent place to start.

- Then mix and match!

## Elevator pitch.

The elevator pitch is a three-part, 30-second introduction to begin every conversation about your work. Did you notice I didn't say *an introduction about your organization*? Because it's not.

Your elevator pitch should sound like:

> The problem
>
> Our solution
>
> The outcome

What most pitches actually sound like:

> Our solution
>
> Our solution
>
> Our solution

No shame.

But the opening and closing statements of your fundraising pitch aren't supposed to be about you. Only talk about your organization and your mission in the middle.

Because remember back to the power of problems from Chapter 1, donors need to lean in. Be invested. Then, your audience also must understand the ultimate payoff for themselves and/or the communities being served.

Here's how to remember this three-part elevator pitch:

**Bad thing**: Lead with the problem.

**Your thing**: Explain the work you do.

**Good thing**: Say the positive outcomes.

The **bad thing** captures attention and frames the conversation. **Your thing** aids in understanding and generates confidence. Then the **good thing** creates urgency and appeals to potential gain.

## CLIENT EXAMPLE: FOOD FOR EDUCATION

- **Bad thing:** *In Kenya, 80% of children in public primary schools have no access to a nutritious school meal. And hungry kids can't learn. (not about them)*

- **Your thing:** *Food for Education mainstreams a school feeding program across Africa by designing a blueprint, operating it, then supporting replication. (about them)*

- **Good thing:** *By 2030, six million children in three African countries will have a school lunch every day. (not about them)*

---

In this case, the opening is short and sweet. In the middle section, the solution is clearly pointing to the fact that this organization has scaled massively and aims for much more growth. Then we back up this scale vision in the closing with a big number.

You'll likely use this piece of mini-storytelling more than any other tool in your platform. In fact, you probably already get this question daily: "Tell me a bit about your organization." So this elevator pitch is where you start.

Always. Like a robot.

**ACTION STEP: WRITE YOUR ELEVATOR PITCH**

The three-part elevator pitch format is: the problem, our solution, the outcome.

- Open with a hook the audience cares about. For example, the problem and/or your reason for being.

- Next, hit them with your specific solution. For example, your mission, interventions, and/or big idea.

- End with a payoff that taps into your listeners' potential gains. For example, the vision, 10-year target, outcomes, uniques, promises, and/or impact data your audience wants to hear.

## Message map.

Building upon the work you just did, think of a message map as your elevator pitch with a turbo boost. It starts with the basics, then shifts gears to deliver detailed, audience-specific insights. You don't just drop your pitch and walk away. You layer in stories and stack up proof points to handle any follow-up questions like a pro.

Another way to think about this tool is to envision a back-and-forth conversation with your ideal donor or target audience. You obviously can't script an entire conversation. And some conversations won't follow this flow.

Still, it gives you a clear priority order for when to say what. And that's all you do: craft the secondary messages that come after the elevator pitch, then tertiary statements to back it all up.

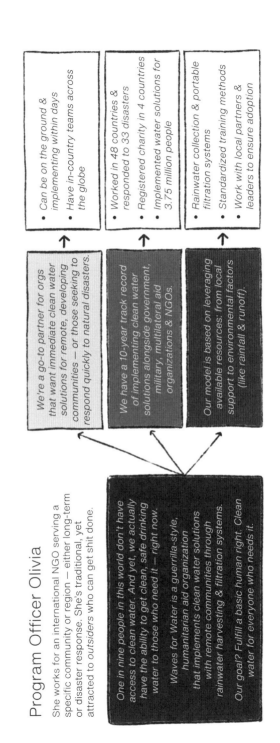

## Program Officer Olivia

She works for an international NGO serving a specific community or region — either long-term or disaster response. She's traditional, yet attracted to *outsiders* who can get shit done.

One in nine people in this world don't have access to clean water. And yet, we actually have the ability to get clean, safe drinking water to those who need it — right now.

Waves for Water is a guerrilla-style, humanitarian aid organization that implements clean water solutions with remote communities through rainwater harvesting & filtration systems.

Our goal? Fulfill a basic human right. Clean water for everyone who needs it.

We're a go-to partner for orgs that want immediate clean water solutions for remote, developing communities — or those seeking to respond quickly to natural disasters.

- Can be on the ground & implementing within days
- Have in-country teams across the globe

We have a 10-year track record of implementing clean water solutions alongside government, military, multilateral aid organizations & NGOs.

- Worked in 48 countries & responded to 33 disasters
- Registered charity in 4 countries
- Implemented water solutions for 3.75 million people

Our model is based on leveraging available resources: from local support to environmental factors (like rainfall & runoff).

- Rainwater collection & portable filtration systems
- Standardized training methods
- Work with local partners & leaders to ensure adoption

FIGURE 20: The Mighty Ally message map tool for client Waves For Water.

## CLIENT EXAMPLE: WAVES FOR WATER

In Figure 20, you'll see one of their audiences (Program Officer Olivia) at the top left. And the Waves For Water elevator pitch in the bottom left box. Then in the middle boxes, their uniques (Chapter 8). On the right, they list a few proof points about each unique.

## ACTION STEP: SKETCH OUT A MESSAGE MAP

Another way to think about this tool is to envision a back-and-forth conversation with your target audience.

- What will you say, what do you want them to think, and what do you want them to do? You obviously can't script an entire conversation. Yet the message map gives you a clear priority order for when to say what.

- And that's all you do: craft the secondary messages that come after the elevator pitch, then create tertiary statements to back it all up.

- One map for each audience.

## Public narrative.

The public narrative is a storytelling framework, created by Harvard professor Marshall Ganz[5] for Barack Obama's presidential campaign. It's now taught by the likes of Acumen and prominent fundraising consultant Jennifer McCrea.

This tool is your guide for every one-way speech. On stage or off, whether you're speaking to a small group, recruiting volunteers, or pitching NGO partners, it gives you the structure to deliver a message that lands, every time.

Outside of the question about what you do (answer: your elevator pitch), the second most common inquiry you'll get as a leader is why you're doing this work.

So to make an impact, weave together three crucial elements in your story:

**The story of self:** Share your *why*. It's not bragging; it's connection. People won't follow you if they don't know what drives you.

**The story of us:** Tap into shared values and common goals. Highlight the stories that resonate, spark action, and build community.

**The story of now:** Don't just ask for support — demand action. Make it clear *what to do* and why this matters right now. Rally people toward a shared vision.

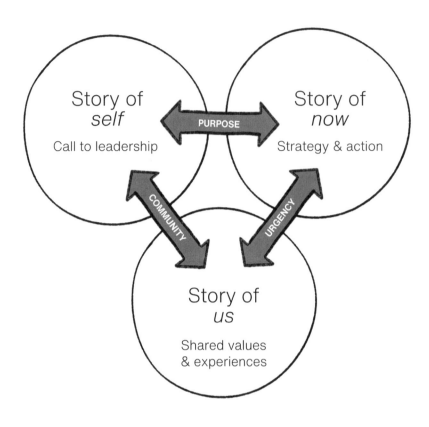

FIGURE 21: The public narrative tool. Credit: Marshall Ganz.

## CLIENT EXAMPLE: COMMUNITY HEALTH IMPACT COALITION

- **Self:** *"In the tumult of my transition to adulthood, when everything was getting grayer and more complex, the right to health stood out as a rare and compelling area of moral clarity. You take an antiretroviral pill, you live. You don't, you die. During that time, I was lucky to have teachers like Dr. Paul Farmer who sharpened that clarity profoundly with their words, writing, and actions."*

- **Us:** *"Many of us have been lucky enough to access adequate healthcare, when we've needed it. We don't know what it is to go without. But illness is universal. We all know how it feels to be sick. To feel weak. To have our lives interrupted and our plans derailed. All education, all creativity, all community, all joy, all meaning — it's only possible when we're first healthy."*

- **Now:** *"We need to get health to everyone. Not because it creates a 10:1 return on investment (though it does), not because our own health depends on our neighbor's health system (though it does \*cough\*). But because it's the foundation for everything that comes after. Community health workers deserve to be salaried, skilled, supervised, and supplied. And our community must act now."*

---

These are just a few of the notes from the CEO's full public narrative, to use when delivering a talk. Not a script, not exact talking points — rather, a framework to remember.

## ACTION STEP: OUTLINE YOUR PUBLIC NARRATIVE

In short: put yourself in the story, show the audience why they should care, and help them know what to do. This is your chance to start telling that old, self-centered founding story differently — in a three-part, public narrative framework.

- What's your **self?** What turning point pushed you to lead?

- What's the **us?** Why should others join you?

- Why **now?** What's the urgency?

## Boilerplate.

Your boilerplate is the ultimate brand snapshot. It's a tool borrowed from public relations, where a boilerplate is a short, standardized paragraph at the end of a press release.

Start with a slightly longer copy block (say, 500 words). Because you'll often need that text for places like your website About page, company LinkedIn profile, or a funder application. Then you can edit down to create shorter versions (like 100, 50, or 25 words) as specific needs arise.

## CLIENT EXAMPLE: JUSTICE DEFENDERS

*Worldwide, three million people are being held in overcrowded prisons without a trial. That's why Justice Defenders — a registered UK charity and a U.S. nonprofit — provides legal education, training, and practice within defenceless communities. Founded in 2007, we work across Africa where prisoners and officers train and provide legal services for themselves and others. This year, 250 of our paralegals and 50 law students will reach 100,000 people in 40 prisons. And this increased capacity promotes more equitable, just, and peaceful societies, in keeping with the UN's 2030 Sustainable Development Goal 16. Visit justicedefenders.org to learn more.*

## ACTION STEP: WORDSMITH YOUR BOILERPLATE

To create a 500-word boilerplate, follow some primary story arc best practices. This structure will feel similar to the elevator pitch:

- First, lead with the problem statement, the people you serve, or your reason for being.

- Second, discuss your interventions and big idea (model), i.e., state clearly what you do.

- Next, boast a little about what makes you unique.

- Then cover some output and outcome impact data to create legitimacy.

- And, just as with the elevator pitch, end with some sort of payoff — like your 10-year target or vision statement. Plus your basic website/contact info, if space allows.

With your messaging and storytelling platform locked, you shouldn't face writer's block when it comes to developing your written words. That's why in Chapter 12, you'll learn more about writing and thought leadership.

Because writing is a fundraising superpower.

# Summary.

1. The messaging and storytelling platform includes your tagline, elevator pitch, message map, public narrative, and boilerplate.

2. Donors want stories first, but eventually need evidence as backup. Because donors give on emotion and justify it with data.

3. Data wrapped in a narrative is 22 times more memorable (science proves it), and data is just a summary of thousands of stories.

4. Messaging is the architecture or framework of what you'll eventually write and say, not all the actual content itself.

5. It's nearly impossible to develop a messaging and storytelling platform without having your theory of change and positioning strategy locked down, first.

# 12. WRITING & THOUGHT LEADERSHIP

Writing is a fundraising superpower.
Ink ignites movements.

Weak writing = weak brand = weak funding.

The reason why should be obvious:

Funding applications = writing.

Positioning strategy = writing.

Theory of change = writing.

Email marketing = writing.

External comms = writing.

Marketing plans = writing.

Internal comms = writing.

Strategic plans = writing.

Video scripts = writing.

M&E reports = writing.

Social media = writing.

Pitch decks = writing.

Speeches = writing.

Websites = writing.

Blogging = writing.

SEO = writing.

PR = writing.

Even creative briefs, a prerequisite for visual design, are writing.

But many nonprofit leaders still cannot translate their big ideas into the written word. Some continue to get tangled up when trying to write clearly about what they do. Especially considering the Global North's unfair dominance of philanthropic wealth, many Global South leaders are writing in a second language, like English.

And most nonprofit leaders aren't experts in communications (as I covered in the introduction). Then their brand falls flat. Their funding isn't maximized. And their desired social justice stalls.

Legendary American activist Representative John Lewis once remarked: "Without storytelling, the civil rights movement would have been like a bird without wings."

So in this chapter you'll learn about **disruptive thought leadership, clear writing = clear thinking,** and **trimming your message** — followed by **five writing tips** to improve your prose.

# Thought leadership: disrupt the norm, draw the donor.

Before we delve into the mechanical side of writing, first you need to get comfortable with a conceptual truth. Being a thought leader means creating conflict. And donors fund the bold, not the bland.

So dare to *turn off* as many people as you *turn on*. Don't simply write about best practices and comfortably speak to the pack. Brave brands are polarizing. And polarization is better than indifference.

Audiences perk up when they hear something contrarian. In the sea of marketing noise — with many nonprofit leaders who sound the same — we all crave a differing perspective.

Even if it provokes us.

That's why a test of courageous positioning is this: some people should love your brand. Many should not. Because the best art divides the audience.

Think of provoking thought leaders like:

- Vu Le, Nonprofit AF

- Tarana Burke, #MeToo

- Malala Yousafzai, Malala Fund

- Greta Thunberg, climate activist

- Dr. Paul Farmer, Partners in Health

- Chimamanda Ngozi Adichie, writer

- Kumi Naidoo, human rights activist

- Peter Singer, The Life You Can Save

Not to mention that challenging the crowd drives innovation.

> *"Fearless, contrarian thinking that polarizes opinion is vital for true thought leadership that can drive change."*
> — *Sarika Goel, corporate coach (Australia)*

So, in your next pitch, presentation, podcast, blog post, or fundraising application — try arguing against an influential idea, powerful institution, or commonly held belief.

See if you can ruffle some feathers. Pique some interest. Aim to be a thought leader who shakes things up, questions the status quo, and inspires others to do the same.

But that will require talking and writing about your work *less* and trying to fundraise *less*. Yes, you heard me right.

Think ideals before deals. Think less time raising funds, and more time raising awareness. Eleanor Roosevelt once said:

**Great minds discuss ideas.**

**Average minds discuss events.**

**Small minds discuss people.**

So here's a version of that maxim for nonprofit leaders:

**Great brands discuss ideas (thought leadership).**

**Average brands discuss their work (marketing communications).**

**Small brands discuss money alone (fundraising and sales).**

It's hard to name a single prominent thought leader in our social sector who didn't create plenty of income opportunities for their organization along the way.

I can testify from experience. As I've grown my own thought leadership through keynote speaking and online writing, I've found that all of the above is true. First, most people love my core message — *More fundraising itself can't fix your fundraising. To get funding, be fundable and findable.* And yet, some do not. Second, as this spiky point of view has become more popular, our qualified income opportunities at Mighty Ally have skyrocketed.

So shift from fundraising to idea-raising. From money trails to movements. And with that concept in mind, now we'll turn your wisdom into words.

## Clear writing: gives poor thinking nowhere to hide.

OK, you want to be a thought leader? Check. You want to write more? Check. But how to start? Here's the second piece of the puzzle:

Don't outsource all your messaging. And don't delegate all your fundraising applications. Because writing is just externalized thinking. Writing is mostly reflection, not typing.

You don't gain clarity, then write. Instead, clarity comes *from* writing. You can always hire a copywriter for extra sizzle. Or get your comms team to add the final creative polish. Or partner with a fundraising firm to repurpose donor appeals.

You can't, however, pay a writer to think for you.

That's why our best brand work at Mighty Ally comes with clients who already publish a lot of content. Then we're extracting vs. dictating truths. Focusing vs. fashioning. And weaving together a messaging and storytelling platform vs. trying to build a narrative from scratch.

So every nonprofit leader (like you!) should produce *some* sort of written thought-leadership content. Like blog posts, white papers, social media, books, op-eds, case studies, annual reports, press releases, research reports, or email newsletters.

Produce any marketing that involves putting thoughts into words. At least get it started and write your own first drafts.

Because "when you write, you find out how sloppy your thinking really is," says journalist Sara Booth.

> *"Most of us don't know how many assumptions we're making, how many terms we're using that we only approximately know the meanings of, how often we jump directly from 'this sounds reasonable to me' to 'this is proven.' But when we write, we have to persuade others. This means we have to define how we got from Point A to Point N. And at that point we often find out that we don't know." — Sara Booth, journalist (United States)*

The bottom line: write your mind, don't rent it out. And pen your vision, don't pawn it. Your true voice isn't for lease.

Now that you're starting to get words on the page, let's talk about tightening them up.

# Trim your message: fatten your funding.

The more you talk and type, the more suspicious you are. Because simplicity speaks truth to donors. But as your complexity increases, your believability decreases.

In fact, Polish scientists used neuroimaging to understand messaging credibility. And they found that excessive wordiness triggered brain regions associated with distrust.[1]

Besides, nobody will read all that you write. And nobody will listen to all that you say. Not our donors, not our partners, not our teams. Because humans scan headlines, we skim subject lines and browse images. But rarely does anyone consume content in full.

Our attention spans are just eight seconds — shorter than a fish.[2] Even when we actively choose to read something online, research shows we spend just 26 seconds looking at it.[3] Similar to books where a 20% completion rate is typical.[4]

> *"Never in the history of humanity have we vomited more words in more places with more velocity. But people keep banging out emails, letters, memos, papers, stories and books like it's 1980. If you want vital information to stick in the digital world, you need to radically rethink — and repackage — how you deliver it."* — Smart Brevity

So donors crave simplicity, not sophistication. And funders flee from complicated fundraising pitches. Even Albert Einstein, one of the smartest humans in history, believed the ultimate form of intelligence is *simple*.

The Global Brand Simplicity Index found:

**Simplicity earns a premium:** 64% of people are willing to pay more for simpler experiences.

**Simplicity builds loyalty:** 61% of people are more likely to recommend a brand because it's simple.

**Simplicity inspires:** 62% of employees at *simple* companies are brand champions vs. only 20% of employees at *complex* companies.

Powerful stuff. And while similar data doesn't exist for nonprofit fundraising specifically, it's easy to apply the same idea to help keep you simple:

- Repeat your main point in speeches.

- Define your mission in eight words or less.

- Get your theory of change on a single page.

- Use clear, jargon-free language in all messaging.

- Craft a pithy tagline that encapsulates your work.

- Streamline donation processes to 2–3 steps or fewer.

- Condense annual report text to impactful infographics.

- Focus on one primary call-to-action in communications.

To be clear, I'm not talking about dumbing down or using sound bites. And short does not mean shallow.

Here are three quick examples for your messaging:

Martin Luther King Jr.'s *I Have a Dream* speech was shorter than a TED Talk. But it's one of the most memorable in history.

The UN's Universal Declaration of Human Rights enshrines the freedoms of all human beings worldwide. Yet each declaration averages just 45 words.

Ernest Hemingway was once challenged to write a story in just six words, or so the legend goes. He penned: "For sale: baby shoes, never worn."

Don't get me wrong. Simple isn't easy. It takes talent and skill to make things simple. Because "simplicity is the ultimate sophistication," said Leonardo da Vinci.

But there's no denying the facts: complexity confuses, simplicity converts. A simple story secures stronger support. And fundraising believability starts with brevity.

And with that brevity, you're well on your way to becoming a better writer. But before you're ready to click *publish*, here's a final set of tips.

# Five writing tips: improve your prose.

**Read a lot:** Not every reader writes, but every writer reads. So to master the written word, you have to consume a lot.

**Just get words on the page:** "A shitty first draft, while not a thing of beauty, is a miracle of victory over nothingness, inertia, bad self-esteem," says the author Anne Lamott.[6] "Secret? Butt in chair."

**Use shorter sentences:** Take half your commas. Replace them with periods.[7]

**Kill your set-up verbs:** Boldly claim your wins. Because set-up verbs add extra words, water down your impact, and weaken your writing. Examples:

- You don't work to improve learning outcomes. *You improve learning outcomes.*

- You don't provide clean water solutions. *You clean water.*

- You don't lobby to change policy. *You change policy.*

- And you don't help save lives. *You save lives.*

**Think impact over intentions:** Similar to killing your set-up verbs, you can claim more credit in your fundraising materials. Instead of always spelling out your full mission and then the results, sometimes you can just state the results part. Like when there's limited space in headlines or sound bites. Why? Results speak louder than actions. And donors perk up when you talk wins over work.

## CLIENT EXAMPLES

*Sabre Education*

- *Mission messaging (the work): Partnering with government to implement play-based learning at scale.*

- *Results messaging (the win): Implementing play-based learning at scale.*

*OceanMind*

- *Mission messaging (the work): Powering enforcement authorities to protect the world's fisheries.*

- *Results messaging (the win): Protecting the world's fisheries.*

*Justice Defenders*

- *Mission messaging (the work): Training paralegals and lawyers to defend defenseless communities.*

- *Results messaging (the win): Defending the defenseless.*

Removing the first *doing verb* allows the second, or the *result verb*, to shine. Not so hard, eh? So look for opportunities to brag about your wins. The outcomes.

Yes, attribution is challenging in the social sector (it takes a village!). And yes, you often want to acknowledge all those partners involved in your work. But funders know your work is complicated and involves many actors — including communities themselves. And your theory of change should acknowledge those partners.

So don't let attribution humility water down your victories. Your impact is often the lead. Make it the star. A slight shift in your donor messaging can do wonders.

Missions get you started. Results get you funded.

> *"Words have power. Words are power. Words could be your power."* — *Mohammed Qahtani, speaker (Saudi Arabia)*

After you take in all this advice, you'll be well on your way to becoming a better writer and thought leader.

But it's not merely what you say and write that matters. The other side of the coin is your visual identity (how you look), and you'll learn how to create one in Chapter 13.

# Summary.

1. Every single element of your brand and fundraising involves writing. So writing is a fundraising superpower.

2. Being a thought leader means creating conflict (and going beyond messaging about your work), so find a stance that polarizes audiences. It's better than indifference.

3. Writing is really just externalized thinking, and clarity comes from writing. So don't outsource all your messaging.

4. Excessive wordiness can trigger brain regions associated with distrust.

5. Brief doesn't mean simplistic.

# 13. VISUAL IDENTITY
## It's OK for nonprofits to look a little slick.

The human brain processes images 60,000 times faster than text,[1] so even a glance at your brand tells your audience much. That's why a seductive visual identity communicates a lot. Before they even read or hear a single line.

In a world where our brains are bombarded with more than 11 million signals[2] — each second — we need every communications advantage we can get. Every edge to ensure that our thinking and messaging lands.

But for some reason, we've come to believe organizations can't look too slick in the social sector. That we actually want to look a little needy. That we shouldn't invest money in branding. That it's somehow OK to have a crummy identity. Because "it's only the impact that matters."

Wrong.

Let's correct the score.

Because bold branding helps maximize your funding, which helps drive impact.

Read on to learn in this chapter **why your visual identity matters, the parts of a branding system,** and **how to create one.** Countless books have been written about design and branding, so this chapter won't cover all those details. But since this topic can intimidate some leaders, here's what you absolutely have to know:

Sharper image. Stronger funding.

What does gift
wrapping say...

...that a paper
bag doesn't?

FIGURE 22: How you look matters for what you say.

## Why visual identity matters.

Your logo isn't your brand, just as the clothes don't make the person. Like people, brand is deeper than how it's represented on a page.

But we all make specific choices on how to dress for a job interview or first date. Because appearance can and does matter. That look is your visual identity. Part of your brand.

A few reasons why how you look matters for what you say:

**Breaking through the noise:** A unique visual identity can set your organization apart from other nonprofits. And ensure that your mission stands out — and stays there — in the minds of potential supporters.

**Fostering trust and credibility:** Gaining the trust of donors, volunteers, and participants is essential. Visual consistency in branding can reassure stakeholders of professionalism, integrity, and attention to detail. Plus, donors believe in nonprofits they recognize.

**Increasing engagement:** Compelling visuals can lead to more social media shares, more event attendance, and more content engagement. A thoughtful visual identity can resonate with local cultures. It can act as a bridge, reflecting cross-over respect and understanding for the communities served.

**A rallying cry for teams and partners:** A solid visual identity can mobilize volunteers and community members around a cause. It creates a sense of belonging, unity, and pride. A stylish identity can attract collaborations and partnerships, greatly amplifying a nonprofit's reach and resources.

*"In the brand world, strategy without design is lifeless, and design without strategy is mute." — Von Glitschka, creative director (United States)*

# The parts of a visual identity system.

You can think of a visual identity in five basic parts:

- Logo

- Color palette

- Typography (as in, fonts)

- Graphic elements (like iconography)

- Photography

The five parts work in totality. Some parts of the identity system will elevate one piece of your brand character. Some will accentuate other traits. So you must focus on the whole.

There's an age-old mantra in the design world that "form follows function." This means that an excellent visual identity isn't just a set of marks that are pleasing to the eye. It should be built on intentional choices, and always be informed by your theory of change and positioning strategy. Every element should have a purpose.

When we work with clients, we find that some nonprofits already have a decent visual identity to build upon. So we're often just refreshing elements that don't work. Some identities we evolve, keeping a few visual equities to tie the old and new systems together. Other organizations need a major overhaul. Nothing is sacred with them. Nothing is spared.

So before we dig deeper, get clear where you are on the spectrum.

*"Design should never say, look at me. It should always say, look at this." — Ma Yansong, architect (China)*

# How to create your visual identity.

Many nonprofits bootstrap the basics of marcom internally. But most of you (myself included) don't have professional graphic designers full-time and in-house. That's why your visual identity work is best left to creative experts, externally, who are versed in design mechanics and translating strategy into visuals.

Depending on your needs and budget, you could engage a creative agency. Or you may have access to a volunteer willing to work pro (or low) bono. Services like Catchafire and Taproot Foundation could also be an avenue to connect with professionals willing to donate their expertise for your cause.

There's no one, perfect way to build a visual identity.

But we use a gated, waterfall process that includes the following steps.

**Create a RACI matrix** (responsible, accountable, consulted, and informed). This RACI will drive internal clarity on who gets to weigh in, and when. That means documenting who is responsible for particular pieces of the project, who is accountable, who isn't as involved but is consulted, then who only gets one-way information. This includes senior leadership and board members. Because nothing derails a creative project more than someone jumping in at the last minute.

Before talking about the visual identity itself, **root the creative in the positioning strategy** work you already completed. Recap where you landed on priority audiences, plus your brand personality character and traits. These previous elements will drive every visual decision from here on out — make sure they're firm in your mind.

Dedicate time to **bring your designer up to speed** on your founding story, theory of change, positioning, and culture. Help them frame their creative vision within a solid organizational strategy.

Next, you need to **look back to your previous and current visual identity**. Think about your logo, colors, typography, graphics, and photography. Plus all your guidelines and templates. You can use a classic RWMC grid (right, wrong, missing, and confused) to note your team's findings, by asking everyone "What's right here?" then documenting that list. "What's wrong here?" then documenting that list. And so on. Most visual identity projects carry over an idea, color, or concept from the old version. These visual consistencies are great ways to ensure that your audiences recognize the refreshed system. Plus, sometimes certain pieces of your identity are simply sacred to you. And that's OK. As long as you name those elements now, before the ideation process begins.

**Then think about any brand in any space.** All creative work builds on what came before. So, the more good ideas you collect, the more you can choose from to be influenced by. Not to mention, nonprofits can learn a lot about branding from the private sector. So let your imagination roam. Whom do you emulate, and why? Name three brands whose visual identity you love. Those that you think could be applicable to your own. Why do you resonate with it? Which elements would you like to carry into your identity?

Now it's time to talk brass tacks: **decide on the actual visual identity assets** you'll create. Of course, there are the logo, colors, and brand guidelines. But you need to ensure you're covering any other needs like PowerPoint or Google Slides templates and email marketing designs. All of these needs will end up in a creative brief where you detail the project needs. From that brief, your designers get to work. So let's be sure you're thinking of everything now.

**Make a few agreements with your creatives**. Most social sector leaders have never been through a formal visual identity process. No shame there. Yet, visual identity is the piece of a brand process where people without creative experience feel most eager to give advice. Because we can all see visuals, it's easy to comment on them. Especially looking at you, Executive Director friends! But, the process can go off track if you don't give agency to the design team. So you should commit to the following:

- Say the problem; let the creative professional find the solution.

- Only those involved in brand strategy get to give feedback on creative.

- Trust the process. They're experts in brand. You're experts in your work.

- Root all your feedback in brand strategy; not personal, subjective opinion.

## Once you have your new visual identity, then what?

You must use it well.

Creating a visual identity only gets you to the starting line. Unfortunately, using it effectively is where many stumble. Logo files are buried in an unknown folder. Employees never download fresh new fonts. Templates get misapplied. That's why we recommend appointing a *brand chief* internally who is responsible for keeping everyone up to date.

And did I mention dozens of times in this book already that everything you produce must be aligned with brand strategy?

*"I always think of my high school piano teacher who once told me, 'Talent, my dear, is much more common than you think. The discipline to practice is rare.' Design is important, but consistency and repetition of a decent design/message may trump. I'll take the songbird that sings the same note, over and over, without looking bored. Great brands don't swerve off message, color, design, or font, so we remember them." — Angela Wier, nonprofit consultant (United States)*

So if you're pushing social change, let your visuals shout it loud. Consistently. Your story is powerful. Ensure that your brand is seen — not just heard.

And one of the most circulated (and important) places where your brand is seen and heard is your pitch deck, which is next in Chapter 14.

# Summary.

1.  Your visual identity includes logo, color palette, typography, graphic elements, and photography (the parts work together in totality).

2.  Since the human brain processes images 60,000 times faster than text, a glance at your visuals says a lot about you as an organization.

3.  There are many reasons why visual identity matters: breaking through the noise, fostering trust and credibility, increasing engagement, and giving your teams and partners a strong rallying cry.

4.  Working with creative teams will be unlike most collaborations that nonprofit leaders are used to — so tools like proper feedback, a RACI matrix, and clear briefs will help you.

5.  Developing a bold visual identity system is only the start — it must be used well.

# 14. PITCH DECK
Reject presentations, embrace conversations.

A wise investor once said that inside every 67-page pitch deck is a useful one-pager struggling to get out. That same venture capitalist later explained this universal truth: nobody likes their time wasted.

> "Good communication is the ability to say the most stuff in the fewest words. Those receiving information skim, skip, and mind-wander far more often than they ask for more." — Morgan Housel, venture capitalist (United States)

This truth is proven with data. DocSend found that investors spend just 3:44 minutes on a pitch deck.[1] So donors snooze through stuffed pitch decks. And wordy pitches are a fundraising repellent.

The best companies and communicators know this fact. And adjust their presentations accordingly. Airbnb's first (and famous) pitch deck had only 14 slides, with 300 words total. It led to an easy $615k seed round in 2009, with another $7.2M coming a year later. Similarly, Mighty Ally once developed an eye health pitch deck to help a client raise billions of dollars. And it was just 15 slides with only a few words per slide.

Then why do nonprofit leaders overly complicate our pitch decks? Perhaps we're just too close to it to simplify. Or perhaps it's just well-intentioned bravado. We like talking about our work and care about the communities we serve.

Regardless of the reason, nonprofits must get better at pitching, if we want to get better at fundraising.

In this chapter you'll learn to **embrace conversations** and **how to create a pitch deck.**

## Embracing conversations: not presentations.

Leaders are accustomed to chasing money and selling their work. Accustomed to the power imbalance with funders, thinking they must impress.

But, as the sales firm Win Without Pitching reminds us, presenting is a tool of swaying, while conversing is a tool of weighing.[2] Through the latter, you determine if both parties would be well served by working together.

A pitch deck is meant for each party to weigh the other: to stimulate interest and further conversation. Not to convey every last detailed aspect of your nonprofit or new idea. And it's certainly not designed to convince. Because presentations build buying resistance, while conversations lower it.

You can follow up with more info if the overview is well received. Or schedule a deep-dive meeting. Then deliver a great proposal, as you'll learn about in Chapter 18. But if the audience loses interest in this critical first impression? Game over.

So spark the chat, not the nap.

Aim for engagement, not escape.

Tease interest, then talk.

> "We must move away from the place where the client sits
> with arms crossed in the role of judge, and we take to
> the stage with song-and-dance in the role of auditioning
> talent. Stars do not audition." — Shannyn Lee, Win
> Without Pitching (Canada)

That's why I say: talk *with* donors. Not *at* donors.

Research has found that collaborating with the prospect is the
second key behavior for achieving funding success — right after
educating them on your work. Not to mention, prospects can
smell desperation.

So whether it's a fundraising or sales meeting, you must break
the habit of trying to convince. Instead, talk *with* donors about a
mutual evaluation of fit.

Here's how, in three golden rules:

**Start by asking questions, keep asking questions:** The better the
questions, the better the answers. Because you'll know how to tailor
your side of the chat. Ask bold questions like "What reservations
do you have?" — so you can address them immediately.

**Only use your pitch deck to spark the conversation:** Then take the deck off-screen. Or, better yet, only send it as a follow-up. I do this myself and watch people's eyes fill with relief, grateful they're not being lulled into yet another PowerPoint nap that day.

**Aim to speak around 40% of the time:** Even if the prospect asks you to present, getting the donor to talk is better. Case in point: Zoom AI apps can track your talk time. And studies show the highest close-rates at a 43/57 talk-to-listen ratio.[3]

Like somebody's wise mother once said — "you have two ears and one mouth for a reason, so shut up and listen." (Especially men.)

Your next meeting isn't a stage performance. It's a dialogue. The future isn't in your slides. It's in your words, and theirs.

Time to flip the script. Literally.

## How to create your pitch deck.

Our pitch deck format below is designed for growth-stage nonprofits. We based it on story arc best practices, learnings from Silicon Valley venture capital, and our years of brand building.

Modify the following five main sections at your own risk — this stuff has been proven. But definitely feel free to rename a section or include the content that serves your nonprofit best. Make it your own.

Here's the ideal format, with a page or two per section.

**Problem or challenge:** Open with a bang (1–2 pages about the issue at hand). Get the audience leaning in, understanding why this conversation matters, and also triggering their primal instinct to either thrive or survive. Important: this piece is not about you! It can include your theory of change problem statement. It often talks about the people being served. And it can be powerful with a statistic or two that quantifies the problem — but doesn't overwhelm. Better yet, tell a story that frames the issue.

**Solution, mission, how it works:** With the proper framing in place, explain your solution, idea, or mission. If it's a pilot or early-stage organization, don't shy away from calling it a hypothesis. This invites the audience into your solution. The *rule of three* can work well here, like three interventions or a three-phase process. Best would be a simple graphic that visually illustrates your work. Remember, save all the nitty-gritty details for later!

**Evidence of impact, about, partners:** Now you've conveyed a problem and a solution. Next, you'll give the audience confidence that your organization can execute well. And that you'd be a trusted recipient of their investment or partnership. This piece can include your impact results to date. Use some typical *about us* language around the team, years in business, and locations. Or possibly about the partners or funders you've worked with so far — to add social proof.

**Vision or desired outcomes:** The final step before the all-important *ask* is telling the audience where you're headed. And getting them excited about the journey ahead. Because nothing motivates people more than bold dreams. Perfect for this element is the 10-year target or vision statement derived from your theory of change. Or, for a more academic audience, you can even speak to long-term outcomes you're measuring.

**Call-to-action, the ask, contact:** Finally, it's time to call the audience to action. Make the ask. Prompt with a question. This is your chance to create urgency (just like the public narrative tool in Chapter 11) — why now is the time and exactly what they can do to join you and your cause. If it's money you need, mention specifics. But also remember the adage: if you ask for money, you'll get advice, and if you ask for advice, you'll get money. So, seek relationships over immediate transactions.

## But what about everything else?

Some investors will want to see financials. Showing your knowledge of the target market or competition is always helpful. Especially important are team bios — since funders most often invest in people instead of specific ideas.

But put all this information in the appendix, so you can flip to it during the conversation. Or send it as a follow-up. Don't crowd the main message and don't delay the back-and-forth dialogue.

Remember: people might give you a few minutes of their time. But, they likely *won't* give you a few minutes of their undivided attention.

There are probably 100 reasons why your organization is great. But people can only remember a few of them after a short pitch. If you just communicate your main points clearly, you'll do better than most.

## Your pitch deck should have a 500-word limit.

Yet, nonprofits can struggle to cut a single line. So what to do? Send a follow-up email with a beefy investment profile or annual report.

Because a pitch deck is not meant for the audience to read verbatim while you speak. If a foundation's eyes are glued to your slides — not you — you've lost their engagement.

Boldness lies in brevity: make every word count.

> *"A pitch should have 10 slides, last no more than 20 minutes, and contain no font smaller than 30 points. This impossibly low number forces you to concentrate on the absolute essentials." — Guy Kawasaki, venture capitalist (United States)*

## Share your downsides.

Here's a comms mind trick from Acumen Academy you can use for your next pitch. Tell the funder reasons why your idea might *not* work. Sharing downsides works well in the appendix. Or after you share your initial slides and start the conversation.

Why? This does five things:

- Surprises them (in a good way), and every good story has suspense.

- Indicates that your idea is big and important enough to potentially fail.

- Shows humility and wisdom, compared to other hubristic leaders pitching.

- Builds trust and shifts the pitch into a two-way collaboration around solutions.

- Lets you address future remedies, and makes them work harder to find objections.

## Use these best practices.

- Animation can be cheesy, so incorporate it sparingly.

- Include contact info on the back page, in case it gets forwarded.

- Pick clear, compelling images. One per slide. Don't stretch them.

- Needless to say, visuals matter. Use your custom fonts and colors.

- Adopt Google Slides vs. PowerPoint — it's better for collaboration.

- Always save your pitch deck as a PDF file before sending over email.

- Spell check! Utilize a tool like Hemingway Editor to improve your writing.

## Customize a version for each priority audience.

You should have one main pitch deck. But, thinking back to your positioning strategy, you can slightly customize the deck for each of the three priority audiences (Chapter 8). Because you'll pitch each audience in somewhat different ways.

Think about the personas and brand promises for each target. Your call-to-action section will definitely be different in each version. How should messaging be tweaked to meet the pains and gains for each audience?

The good news about tweaking your pitch deck messages for specific audiences: you'll then use a very similar line of thinking on your website.

And that's coming up next in Chapter 15, because your website is your best (or worst!) fundraiser.

# Summary.

1.  Your pitch deck should contain the following sections: problem, solution, evidence, vision, and call-to-action.

2.  It should only be 10–15 pages in length, with about a 500-word limit (if well-funded corporate startups can do it, you can too).

3.  A pitch deck is only meant to spark a conversation, not to be a one-way presentation.

4.  Research has found that donor prospects like to collaborate in meetings — in fact, it's the number-two driver of pitch success, right after educating them.

5.  If you put too many words in your deck, the donor's eyes will be on your slides and not you — then you've lost.

# 15. WEBSITE STRATEGY

Your website is your best (or worst!) fundraiser.

One of our first clients was a nonprofit that ran a summer camp for less-privileged kids in the Southern United States. They had a history of impact along with a unique racial equality mission. But a horrible website strategy. Paid camp registrations fueled their earned revenue model. Yet the naive pro-bono web firm had slapped *Donate* and *Volunteer* buttons everywhere. That's what nonprofits are supposed to ask for, right?

Unfortunately, the site didn't encourage visitors to sign up for camp — the vital business goal. And millions of dollars were lost over time.

This story illustrates perfectly how your website is your best (or worst) funding employee. And why your site is the most critical communications channel for any nonprofit. Because it raises money 24 hours a day, 365 days a year. Your homepage is the front door of your brand.

Then why are websites often a disastrous afterthought? Web strategy can feel too complicated. Good design and content seem expensive. Or leaders say there's no time or team.

Thanks to out-of-the-box website solutions, building a site has become remarkably cheap from a design and technology standpoint. You can find talented freelancers anywhere and activate them quickly. It seems that the strategic connective tissue is what's really missing.

> "*A website strategy is a plan of action that directs the content, layout, and funnel on your website. It considers your business objectives and then outlines the ways your website can align with those plans to actively help you reach your goals.*" — *Raubi Marie Perilli, website strategist (United States)*

So here's our formula for nonprofits (which we use ourselves!). Remember 1-3-5-7-9, which you'll learn more about in this chapter: **one call-to-action, three audience goals, five sitemap pages, seven homepage sections,** and a **$9,000 USD average budget.** Plus a **website strategy brief** to pull it all together.

# 1 call-to-action.

Your website strategy starts by determining the most critical, one call-to-action on the site. In essence, if you boil it all down, what's the site for in the first place?

Let's cut the clutter. Imagine that your website had just one page with one logo, one photo, one paragraph, and one button. What would that button do?

Don't forget what happens once a web visitor clicks. Yes, bring the horse to water. But ensure that it can drink, by optimizing your forms and technical features.

*"It's much easier to double your business by doubling your conversion rate than by doubling your traffic."* – Jeff Eisenberg, advertising executive (United States)

## CLIENT EXAMPLES

*Justice Defenders: Join the Defenders*

*Buffalo Bicycles: Purchase*

*JUST: Join the Community*

---

For a lot of nonprofits or charities, this most critical call-to-action will be just one word: donate. With Justice Defenders, it's a big red button in the navigation that stays fixed as you scroll, the first button you see on the homepage hero, and even repeated in the bottom picture. For social enterprises that sell a product, the call-to-action may be Shop Now if you have e-commerce. Or, as with our client Buffalo Bicycles (a division of World Bicycle Relief that sells through distribution partners), it can be another sales-related call-to-action. The JUST website repeatedly invites women to sign up and click the main call-to-action button.

## ACTION STEP: DETERMINE YOUR CALL-TO-ACTION

The point here is to identify the main desired conversion and then do everything possible to get people to take that action. Don't try to convert too many people into too many paths simultaneously. A confused mind always says no.

- Pick one call-to-action.

- What should the main button say?

- And what should it link to?

# 3 audience goals.

A single call-to-action is great, but it's not enough. Your website must juggle multiple objectives and reach different audiences. Even if you have a single, primary call-to-action (from the previous step), you can address these three audiences in more indirect ways. Like copy and subpages.

You should already know — going back to your value propositions in Chapter 8 — the top three audiences you're trying to reach with your brand. For example, you might target high-net-worth donors, bilateral funders, and ministry officials. Therefore, your website strategy should serve three audience goals: one macro goal for each target.

Go back to your positioning personas and ask, *what would they want from our website?* Then you can make deliberate decisions with your sitemap and homepage sections below.

## CLIENT EXAMPLE: VEGA COFFEE[1]

- *Discerning, savvy customer: Easily find and shop in order to select desired coffee and frequency, then complete purchase.*

- *University food-service decision-maker: Understand the basics of the Vega model to reinforce the price/ quality brand promise.*

- *Brand ingredient buyer: Perceive Vega as an established brand with clout that can help improve their own brand's perception.*

---

While our client wanted to sell to direct customers first and foremost, we also had to build a site that spoke to their B2B audiences. That's similar to many clients with a Donate button for individuals, but also needing to attract institutional funders.

**ACTION STEP: NAME YOUR AUDIENCE GOALS**

Your three priority audiences from the positioning strategy almost always carry over into the website strategy.

- List them and ask, what do we hope for each to accomplish on the site? Then write out the audience goals in one sentence, max.

- Remember back to brand promises: these goals should be mostly about helping them achieve gains or reduce pains. Not as much about you.

# 5 sitemap pages.

A sitemap maps out your website's journey. It's the outline behind your navigation menu, whether your sitemap is a detailed flowchart, a spreadsheet, or a quick sketch on paper. Whatever form it takes, a sitemap helps you plan how visitors move through your content, page by page.

We recommend a primary navigation of five sitemap pages. Give or take a page, including your main conversion page, like *Contact Us* or *Donate*. We say this because most nonprofits don't have significant, enterprise-level websites requiring dozens of pages. And an average website visitor will only spend 90 seconds on your site. So giving them too many pages is just overwhelming visually. Especially considering that each of your five subpages can contain upwards of seven sections like your homepage (which we'll get to in a moment). That's already plenty of content to scroll through!

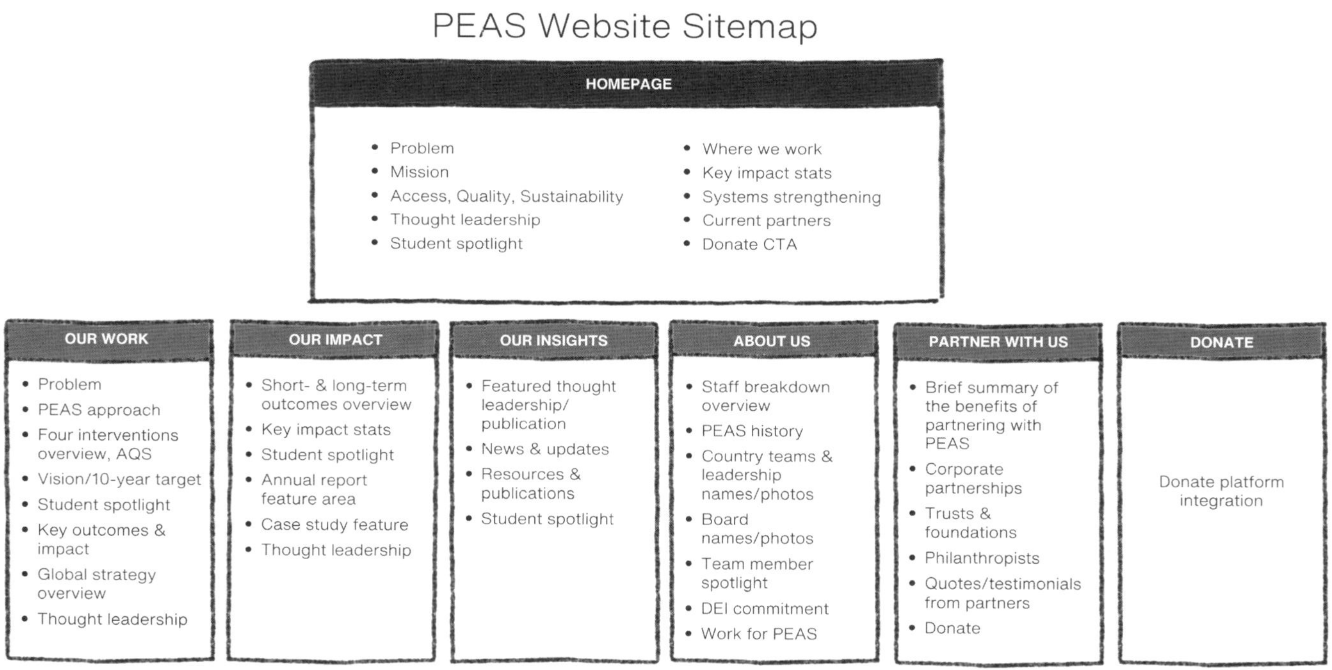

# PEAS Website Sitemap

**HOMEPAGE**
- Problem
- Mission
- Access, Quality, Sustainability
- Thought leadership
- Student spotlight
- Where we work
- Key impact stats
- Systems strengthening
- Current partners
- Donate CTA

**OUR WORK**
- Problem
- PEAS approach
- Four interventions overview, AQS
- Vision/10-year target
- Student spotlight
- Key outcomes & impact
- Global strategy overview
- Thought leadership

**OUR IMPACT**
- Short- & long-term outcomes overview
- Key impact stats
- Student spotlight
- Annual report feature area
- Case study feature
- Thought leadership

**OUR INSIGHTS**
- Featured thought leadership/ publication
- News & updates
- Resources & publications
- Student spotlight

**ABOUT US**
- Staff breakdown overview
- PEAS history
- Country teams & leadership names/photos
- Board names/photos
- Team member spotlight
- DEI commitment
- Work for PEAS

**PARTNER WITH US**
- Brief summary of the benefits of partnering with PEAS
- Corporate partnerships
- Trusts & foundations
- Philanthropists
- Quotes/testimonials from partners
- Donate

**DONATE**
- Donate platform integration

FIGURE 23: A sketch version of the PEAS sitemap, originally created in Google Sheets.

## CLIENT EXAMPLE: PEAS

In our website strategy work with PEAS, the sitemap was nothing fancy. It was just listing out all the pages on the site. Then roughly detailing the type of content that will go into each page. Some web designers might prefer a full wireframe for each page. The best designers will want the creative freedom to take this sitemap and bring the page to life.

## ACTION STEP: LIST OUT YOUR SITEMAP

What are your five main pages? And what are they called?

- Common ones include About Us, Our Work, Impact, and Contact Us.

- If you require subpages, limit those to five as well for 10 total.

# 7 homepage sections.

Your homepage is essentially the front door of your brand. So spend more of your website strategy time here, because most visitors will see your homepage, plus maybe 1–2 other pages. Visitors are gone if you don't hook them right away and give them a clear path to proceed.

You can use a wireframe to sketch these homepage sections. Think of a wireframe as the bones of your website. It maps out your content's layout and guides user flow, ensuring that every piece has its place. Aim for seven sections on your homepage. Too few, and you'll miss key details. Too many, and you risk overwhelming visitors with a cluttered experience.

So whether you write out your homepage wireframe in a text document or use a visual format, here are the standard seven sections:

**Header:** Lead with the problem you're solving and who you're serving. This hero area hooks the visitor and sets the stage for what's to come.

**Brand promise:** Explain the value proposition of your product or service. This text can be your mission or reason from the theory of change.

**About:** Now, let the visitor *meet the guide* behind the work. Share a bit about your organization so they'll feel connected to the cause.

**The model:** Here you'll reassure the visitor that the guide (you) has a plan or impact process. This piece can be your main 3–4 interventions.

**Impact:** Now it's time to brag. At this point, you showcase your success to date. Impact stats are ideal — outcomes are better than outputs.

**Authority:** If the impact data hasn't convinced the visitor to convert, use testimonials and/or logos here to give social proof.

**Footer:** Put everything else in this bottom section. Like the email signup (unless it's your main call-to-action!), social icons, and other content not important enough for the main navigation menu at the top.

Since we practice what we preach, see this homepage format in real life at *mightyally.org*. Then with those sections in place, your homepage can act like a standalone one-pager or digital elevator pitch (like our site does). It will tell a complete brand story, without the viewer even needing to click.

One page, one purpose: captivate instantly.

---

## ACTION STEP: SKETCH THE HOMEPAGE SECTIONS

- There are great tech tools, like Balsamiq and Marvel, if you want to geek out.

- But your wireframe does not have to be complicated. You can effectively sketch out a homepage using just a notepad or whiteboard and the seven sections above.

- It's the thinking that matters, not something flashy.

---

# $9k USD average budget.

How much does a website cost? That's like asking the price of a car or a house.

It all depends. Want something basic? You'll pay less but get fewer features. Looking for something high-end? Be ready to invest more. Quality and cost go hand in hand. And remember: this website is the front door for your brand, so don't skimp on the investment.

For this reason, complete your website strategy process by determining your budget. Because all the decisions above need to be grounded in what you can actually afford. And budget is the main question that a web development firm will want to ask.

High-end sites from quality web shops run $20,000–$40,000 USD. Though sometimes you can get one for as little as $2,500 USD for a very basic website from a freelancer on a platform like Squarespace. So on average, nonprofits can get a decent website designed and developed for around $9,000 USD.

It's key to note.

This budget range assumes you have your theory of change, positioning, branding, website strategy, and content all in place. Plus, you can't continue past this web strategy process (or get this kind of average budget) without having locked down the right messaging and images. Content is queen.

All this brand strategy (like what this book is all about!) takes months and is truly what makes or breaks a good website. The budget levels above apply to the tactical side of website design, coding, and launch *alone*. Not all preceding brand.

# Pulling it all together: website strategy brief.

The website strategy brief consists of your master plan in motion. Your web strategy brief should contain the 1-3-5-7-9 formula above, at the very least. It can also include some additional strategic thinking and technical details. Like these optional sections:

**RWMC:** Use this tool like we did in the visual identity chapter. Gather the team and document what's right, wrong, missing, and confused with your existing website. This retrospective on the current state of affairs will be invaluable in developing the new site. So include these notes in the website strategy brief.

**Landscape analysis:** Don't hesitate to look around at the competitors and collaborators. Reference those identified during your positioning work to see what others are doing on the web. You can use another RWMC list to capture what you like and dislike about other organizations' websites.

**Analytics review:** Take advantage of tools like Google Analytics to analyze performance of the current site. Look to see where users come from around the world. What sources drove them there? What are the most popular pages they visit, the devices they're using, and where they drop off?

**Content requirements:** This website strategy brief is your chance to identify any new copy or multimedia needs beyond your current content. Maybe you want to add a blog — then it's time to write. You might have sketched a big video on your homepage — do you have one? You get the point.

**Technical requirements:** You must consider and document all the functional specifications of the new site. For instance, donation platforms, CRM integrations, email signup code, ecommerce capabilities, or custom features such as searchable databases.

This isn't just a static document. Rather, it's a dynamic guide, ensuring a smooth handoff to developers and guiding every phase of your website's creation.

With the website strategy brief complete, it's off to the races! Time to hand it off to the website design and development team — whether that's internal or a third-party firm.

So go forth and launch. Then study the analytics, optimize, lather, rinse, repeat.

> *"A bad website is like a grumpy salesperson." — Jakob Nielsen, web consultant (Denmark)*

With your website optimized, you'll be ready for the final chapter of this marketing communications section: corporate social responsibility.

Because that's where money meets marketing.

# Summary.

1. Your website strategy can use our 1-3-5-7-9 formula: one call-to-action, three audience goals, five sitemap pages, seven homepage sections, and a $9,000 USD average budget.

2. A website is by far your brand's most important marcom touchpoint (it raises money 24 hours a day, 365 days a year), though it often becomes an afterthought.

3. Your homepage is of utmost importance (because many audiences will only see it, plus 1–2 other pages). So ensure that it tells a complete story.

4. Countless website builders and online tools make creating a website easier (and cheaper) than ever before, so it's the website strategy that still seems to be missing.

5. The website strategy brief is where you pull together items in the 1-3-5-7-9 formula (plus a few optional pieces) before handing off the project to a website designer and/ or developer.

# 16. CORPORATE PARTNERSHIPS

Corporate social responsibility:
where money meets marketing.

I know, I know.

You social sector purists out there simply loathe capitalism. You curse the private sector for the ills it has caused (I sometimes curse it too). And the very idea of partnering with corporations makes you squirm.

That's somewhat fair. But here's the tough love:

Big companies aren't going anywhere. Besides, it's presumptuous to think that one sector alone can solve poverty and injustice.

> *"In terms of power and influence, you can forget the church, forget politics — there is no more powerful institution in society than business. The business of business should not be about money, it should be about responsibility. It should be about public good, not private greed." — Anita Roddick, human rights activist (England)*

Yet our sector thinks of corporate social responsibility (CSR) as merely a donor audience for money. But CSR is the only thing in this entire book that's *both* a funding source *and* a marketing machine. That's why CSR is in this marketing section, and why it should be about far more than just donations.

Because your corporate partners are brand megaphones. A source of free resources and tools. An extension of your team.

If you focus only on the money, you miss valuable opportunities to grow your brand, tap into expertise, and gain new resources.

CSR partnerships should also be mutually beneficial. Again, too often they're not. And corporates are left underwhelmed. So when a shiny new nonprofit comes along, the corporation switches partners. There was little driving value in its direction.

Nonprofits beg corporations for money, desperate for any funding. And for-profit companies do often donate, pulling cash from their overflowing coffers. We're conditioned to expect this dance. It's ingrained in our sector, underscored by scarcity mindsets, upheld by power imbalances, and cemented by inequitable relationships with funders.

But it doesn't have to be this way. The relationships brokered between for-impact and for-profit organizations can be a powerful, mutually beneficial machine.

Like any other marcom activity, corporate partnerships don't happen overnight. But they can and *should* be considered part of your long-term success strategy. These partnerships generate both tangible and intangible returns.

Shared value — a term coined by Michael E. Porter and Mark Kramer[1] — can structure the relationship between for-profit and nonprofit. Instead of creating net-new initiatives for delivering on social good, companies can work alongside existing organizations. They can trade value for value and share in the positive outcomes.

This meaningful shared value conversation allows you to elevate and differentiate your brand.

So channel your inner Robin Hood. And in this chapter, you'll learn **how to create your CSR pitch** the right way, along with four client examples.

CSR offers much more than money

FIGURE 24: Corporates are a funding source and a marketing machine.

# How to create a shared value CSR pitch.

The good news is that if you've created a pitch deck (per Chapter 14), much of the format is the same. The biggest difference is that here we're introducing our idea of CSR partnership pillars. This concept is probably new for most leaders, so let's break it down.

Below are the four main ways that *you get* (as the nonprofit) and *they get* (as the corporate) in a genuine, shared-value partnership. When approaching a potential corporate partner about CSR, remember to structure your two-way relationship around all four Ps: philanthropy, platform, people, and product.[2]

## Philanthropy (financial donations).

**You get:** Thoughtful, strategic, aligned grants. A savvy injection of much-needed capital that yields substantial social change returns.

**They get:** A trusted home to invest their mandated giving. Clear ROI and impact reporting. A connection to where the money is going and the difference it's making.

## Platform (storytelling and promotion).

**You get:** A potentially massive new audience for which to broaden your reach. And new marcom channels to amplify your story.

**They get:** Strengthened brand positioning and powerful differentiation. And the ability to tell a purpose story that goes well beyond surface-level cause marketing.

## People (employee engagement).

**You get:** People power in the form of volunteers and expertise. Exponential growth in the size of your team, without the overhead burden.

**They get:** Employee engagement via integrated learning and skills-based volunteer opportunities. A happier staff by nurturing autonomy, mastery, and purpose.

## Product (in-kind giving).

**You get:** Free resources and tools, for both internal team productivity and external impact with communities in great need.

**They get:** To leverage their core business in the service of others. And also to integrate their product into the fabric of a purpose platform to yield insights, returns, and tremendous value.

# CLIENT EXAMPLES

### Philanthropy (financial donations).

Lwala Community Alliance has a multi-pronged partnership with the corporate side of Tivity Health, its nonprofit Health eVillages, and even the CEO's personal fund — the Tramuto Foundation. For large corporations, philanthropic money will often flow through their foundation or even a wealthy executive's personal office.

### Platform (storytelling and promotion).

Waves For Water has partnered with the global travel brand Tumi for years. Besides funding, Tumi helps capture images, stories, and videos. It then broadcasts this content across its digital channels. It's a win/win. Tumi's brand marketing team promotes core attributes of adventure and exploration, while Waves For Water reaches vast new audiences.

### People (employee engagement).

Reach a Hand Uganda is a sexual and reproductive health and rights (SRHR) nonprofit in Uganda. Lucky Bloke is an international condom retailer with vast expertise around safe-sex practices. Instead of just donating money and product, Lucky Bloke spent time with the RAHU team — knowledge sharing around the latest trends in SRHR. And vice versa.

### Product (in-kind giving).

Ubuntu Life is a Kenyan nonprofit that has brokered a mutually beneficial partnership with the African restaurant chain Java House. Through Ubuntu Life's social enterprise, they sell co-labeled bottled spring water and coffee sleeves to Java House. And Java House provides industrial cooking products for Ubuntu's own cafe.

After you get your partnership pillars in order, it's time to develop your CSR pitch deck. Again, if you've done all the work on your standard pitch deck from Chapter 14, you can re-use most of it.

Here's the formula:

**The problem:** Open with a bang: 1–2 pages about the issue at hand. Get the audience leaning in, understanding why this work matters, and triggering their primal instinct to either thrive or survive. Important: this piece is not about your organization!

**Solution or mission:** With the proper framing in place, spend 2–3 pages explaining your solution, idea, or mission. The rule-of-three can work well here, like three interventions or a three-phase process. Best would be a graphic that visually illustrates your work.

**Evidence and about:** Next, give the audience confidence that your organization can execute well. This piece can include your impact results. And some typical *about us* language. Or possibly about the partners or funders you've worked with so far — to add social proof.

**Vision:** The final step before having an open discussion is telling the audience where you're going. And getting them excited about joining the journey ahead. Ideal for this element is the 10-year target or vision statement from your theory of change.

**Partnership pillars:** Now shift the conversation to your potential CSR partnership. And introduce the concept of shared value. That means how you structure corporate partnerships via these four pillars: philanthropy, people, platform, and product.

**CSR examples:** Next you need to show that you've successfully pulled it off. So showcase 2–3 case studies of your most impactful corporate partners to date. If you're just starting on your two-way corporate-partner journey, at least display the logos of corporates you've engaged with in the past.

**Call-to-action:** Finally, make the ask. Give them contact information. Prompt a question. This is your chance to create urgency — why now is the time and exactly what they can do to join you and your cause.

See how this works?

Not only is the partnership multifaceted (and much more than just money). It's delivering two-way value, them to you and you to them. That's the hallmark of this four Ps framework.

And with this framework down, you deserve another pat on the back. Because you've completed this book's Part Two: Be Findable. And you should now know how to occupy a distinct space in the minds of your ideal funders, and routinely communicate your promises to them.

Just like after the first part, you'll get a quick check-in quiz shortly. Then you'll be ready for Part Three: Get Funding.

# Summary.

1. The CSR corporate partnerships pitch includes four Ps: philanthropy, people, platform, and product.

2. Despite many nonprofit leaders loathing capitalism and all things private-sector, "there is no more powerful institution in society than business."

3. CSR partnerships are often one-way, from the corporate to the nonprofit. But they should embody the spirit of collaborative benefits.

4. A CSR pitch is much like your typical pitch deck. The difference is that you have a slide about your four Ps and then another slide for previous corporate examples.

5. Shared value is a concept defined by Shared Value Initiative as "policies and operating practices that enhance the competitiveness of a company while simultaneously advancing the economic and social conditions in the communities in which it operates." Basically, a win/win.

# PART THREE: GET FUNDING

Gain new donors and keep existing funders by reconsidering the traditional fundraising lifecycle.

# Friendly warning.

Did you buy this book and skip to this Get Funding section, because you think you don't have time for all the upfront stuff? You sly one, you. The whole point of the book is that more fundraising itself can't fix your fundraising. To get funding, be fundable and findable.

Or did you recently complete Part One: Be Fundable and Part Two: Be Findable? And you're excited to keep going? Well, that's awesome but... let's pause for a quick gut check to see if your brand is fundable *and* findable yet.

I'll give you 10 brief statements. These statements cover what you should have achieved by reading and implementing Part Two. So rank your organization on a scale of 1 to 5, where 1 is *weak/don't know* and 5 is *strong*.

## Positioning strategy.

- We can name at least five competitors or collaborators, and understand how we compare to peers across multiple dimensions.

- The factors that make us unique (differentiators) are authentic, important to constituents, and provable — and our staff can recite them to donors.

- We know the top three priority audiences we wish to reach with our brand and have documented their needs, desires, pains, and gains.

- Our products and programs have compelling brand promises (value propositions), and we can tell each priority audience what's in it for them.

- Our brand character, traits, and tradition are set, and this brand personality comes out strongly in all our marketing communications.

## Marketing communications.

- The brand's visual identity (logo, colors, fonts, imagery, and photography) is documented, distinctive, and applied across all marketing channels.

- Our messaging is powerful and resonates in both verbal and written communications — and the team can share our story using the same voice.

- We have prioritized marketing channels in a written comms plan that is updated, resourced, and measured.

- Our website is highly effective in both form (design and storytelling) and function (donations, sales, or email/social growth).

- We use corporate partnerships (CSR) to build our brand through their people, platform, products, and philanthropy.

# How to assess your scores.

Total your points, then divide by 10 to get your average. Our clients average a 3 out of 5 for the questions above. But the goal is a 4.5. That's just 90% in school grade terms. We're not even aiming for a perfect 5.0 or 100%.

So if you're not there yet, really consider putting in the work and first worry about being fundable and being findable. Then move on to Part Three: Get Funding.

Sound good? Now that I've said my piece — off my podium — let's continue into Part Three. It begins with your donor acquisition.

P.S. — Before we dive into Part Three, pause. As I told you before Part Two, you've continued to do the work. Page by page. Exercise by exercise.

In fact, you're now finished with all of the Action Steps in this book. So you've completed most of what it takes to build a clear, compelling nonprofit brand that maximizes your funding and advances social justice.

The rest of this book journey will cement your knowledge and strengthen all you've gained. Because Part Three is about brand mindsets and attitudes with your donors.

You may not have thought you'd be here — equipped with these tools and this confidence. But you are.

So keep climbing.

# DONOR ACQUISITION

Change how you think about nurturing and asking new donors with these brand mindsets.

Funders aren't livestock or land. Or any other items we commonly *acquire*.

Because the definition of the word "acquire" is *to buy or obtain an asset or object*. So calling it *acquisition* objectifies the entire fundraising experience and creates an imbalanced and inferior tone within your organization.

> "At best we acquire the name of a person with a giving history but that person does not know us. Even if we successfully solicit a gift, we still haven't acquired a donor. We've caused a generous person to take a tentative step in our direction. They are never ours." — Jim Langley, fundraising consultant (United States)

In this section, you'll learn more about donor acquisition: **why the term is wrong,** why I've omitted **identification and qualification,** and **how brand/marketing/fundraising fit together.** Then we'll look deeper at parts of donor acquisition in Chapters 17 and 18.

# Donor *acquisition*: wrong term, wrong focus.

There are about 32,500,000 search results for the term *donor acquisition*. Acquisition and retention are the two ways that we (in the philanthropic and business worlds) have been taught to raise money. And acquisition is the tactic that leaders default to when times are tight.

Yet, there are three problems with the terminology itself and how that terminology shapes our fundraising.

## It's dehumanizing.

Every one of your donors is a human on the other end (obviously). From small online givers to institutional grantmakers. So the typical practice of acquisition oversimplifies all the complex relationships involving trust, values alignment, and mutual benefits.

"Prospective donors crave organic connection and impactful collaboration," says Lisa Greer (a major donor herself) in her book, *Philanthropy Revolution*. But "donating to charities feels onerous, dehumanizing, disrespectful, manipulative, and just exhausting."

## It's a marathon, not a sprint.

The acquisition mindset promotes short-term thinking. And leads nonprofits to prioritize immediate donations vs. long-term donors.

So the cliché in our sector about *friendraising* might be a bit cheesy, but it's the right idea. Because you never would say that you need to acquire friends. Or acquire a spouse. Or acquire a community. No, these relationships grow over time.

### It's being fundable (first) that gets funding.

Obsessing over donor acquisition puts your energy on the wrong things. It makes nonprofit leaders push fundraisers to do more, more, more outreach and campaigns and awareness raising.

Instead, your foremost focus should be on getting fundable and findable. First. And, like the famous comedian Steve Martin once told rookie comics trying to break through the noise, "be so good they can't ignore you."

Or in the social sector, perhaps it's more like, *be so good for participants/beneficiaries that donors can't ignore you.*

That excellence will drive far more money than any marketing plan. Any publicity gimmick. Any flashy communications campaign. Or any donor acquisition ideas you might have.

**Because it's easier to make things people want,
than to make people want things.**[1]

Brace yourself.

No psychological tactics or messaging maneuvers will convince customers or donors to give you money, if your stuff isn't worthy.

So how do you create impact, programs, and products that people want to support? How do you be so good that they can't ignore you?

You begin with brand strategy. You start with at least a theory of change (your brand). Next, your strategic plan (your brand). Then positioning strategy (again your brand). Even if you don't do an ounce of marketing communications (also your brand).

Then you get to work. Making things people want. Creating impact. Becoming unignorable. And fundraising wins will follow.

That's brand building. And that's why we should think of it as donor building too. Not as donor acquisition. Because donors are people, not prey.

Stop the hunt.

> *"The relationship must be an equation that adds value to both of you. You have to be clear about the arrival point, but you cannot lose sight of the path. Because that is where the learning is, that is where the revelations occur."*
> — *Marta Lucia de la Cruz Federici, nonprofit alliances coordinator (Colombia)*

## Donor identification and qualification: where are they?

The astute reader will notice that I've skipped two sections of the old-school donor lifecycle: identification and qualification.

Why? As I said in the introduction, this is not a traditional fundraising book.

But here's a refresher on the classic donor cycle (or donor journey, some call it) because as you'll soon see: cultivation, solicitation, stewardship, and engagement all depend on your brand.

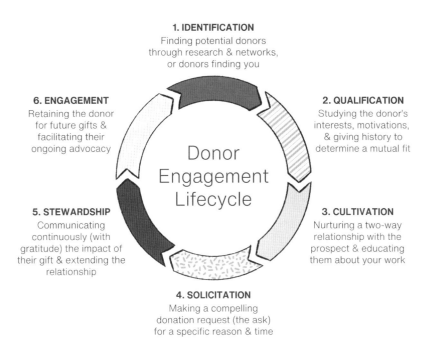

**1. IDENTIFICATION**
Finding potential donors
through research & networks,
or donors finding you

**6. ENGAGEMENT**
Retaining the donor
for future gifts &
facilitating their
ongoing advocacy

**2. QUALIFICATION**
Studying the donor's
interests, motivations,
& giving history to
determine a mutual fit

Donor
Engagement
Lifecycle

**5. STEWARDSHIP**
Communicating
continuously (with
gratitude) the impact of
their gift & extending the
relationship

**3. CULTIVATION**
Nurturing a two-way
relationship with the
prospect & educating
them about your work

**4. SOLICITATION**
Making a compelling
donation request (the ask)
for a specific reason & time

FIGURE 25: The typical donor engagement lifecycle.

The first two steps — identification and qualification — really have nothing to do with brand communications. There are countless books and blogs and experts to help in those areas. So I won't teach you how to research potential funders, conduct donor diligence, or create prospect lists.

That said, before you even think about building a brand to acquire donors, you need to understand which donors are out there. And once you *do* acquire your ideal donors, you'll learn more in Chapter 20 that having a funding-type focus is also critical for donor retention.

I've said enough about why this section of the book isn't about traditional fundraising outreach. So it's worth repeating: brand

and marketing communications and fundraising *do* fit together. We've covered the topic of brand in the intro, then marketing in the previous section, so now let's move on to how they both intersect with fundraising.

## Brand leads: then marketing speaks and fundraising follows.

As nonprofit leaders attempt to acquire donors, it's common to assign the task to your communications team. Or vice versa, it's common to delegate brand work to your fundraising staff.

However, your brand is not a fundraising function. Brand doesn't belong to your comms team. And brand is not the same thing as marketing.

Yes, brand, marketing communications, and fundraising are certainly interconnected. But brand is owned by your leadership. Marketing is owned by your comms team. And fundraising is an entirely separate endeavor.

Here's the breakdown:

**Brand:** Identifying your distinctive DNA in a crowded world. It's crafting your unique organizational fingerprint.

**Marketing:** Broadcasting this DNA to your audiences. It's the process of making your fingerprint recognizable.

**Fundraising:** Ensuring the needed supplies to carry out your DNA's mission. It provides the resources to leave your fingerprint mark.

In other words:

Brand lights the match. Marketing fans the flames. Fundraising fuels the fire. Brand sets the stage. Marketing performs the play. Fundraising fills the seats.

All three are critical. But brands require precise, ongoing management. Not from junior comms staff. From the top leadership down.

Don't just take my word for it.

> *"Instead of having responsibility for the brand reside within the marketing, communications, or development department, responsibility for the brand as a key strategic asset resides with the entire executive team. Rather than focusing on fundraising as the objective of the brand, the new paradigm places the brand in service of the mission and social impact." — The Brand IDEA (a book co-written by a current nonprofit CEO and former funder at DRK Foundation)*

That's why every nonprofit leader is — by default — a brand builder.

Embrace it.

Another thing to embrace? It's your job (and actually everyone's job!) to cultivate donors. That's one of a few things we'll cover next in Chapter 17.

# Summary.

1. The traditional concept of acquisition dehumanizes the entire fundraising experience, focuses too much on short-term gains, and glosses over the fact that being fundable matters more.

2. No donor campaigns will matter (or raise money) if your impact isn't there or is unclear or you're not fundable. Because more fundraising itself can't fix your fundraising.

3. It's easier to make things people want, than to make people want things.

4. The first two steps in the donor lifecycle — identification and qualification — are the jobs of fundraising. Not brand communications. So they're not covered in this book.

5. Your brand is not a fundraising function. Brand doesn't belong to your comms team. And brand is not the same thing as marketing.

# 17. CULTIVATION
## The first step in fundraising is not fundraising.

A major philanthropy publication had finally said it. Fundraising folks were coming around to the truth. An expert fundraiser admitted: the first step in fundraising *isn't* fundraising.

I read the article titled *The Three Pillars Supporting Long-term Fundraising Success* by Eric Streiff in *Philanthropy Daily* and was pleased as punch. Because the article reinforced our *brand first, funding second* point of view. In the frantic scramble for donor dollars, most nonprofits skip the starting line:

Brand.

That's why — as we continue this Get Funding section and talk about cultivation — it's worth repeating: more fundraising itself can't fix your fundraising. To get funding, be fundable and findable.

> *"The success of [fundraising] hinges on three core elements: brand awareness, donor retention, and donor engagement."* — *Eric Streiff, philanthropy writer (United States)*

Brand awareness is the beginning of your donor relationships. Donor retention harnesses the power of long-term commitment. Donor engagement builds a community of active advocates.

If even the philanthropy gurus tell you to start with brand, it's time to set a new pace for your organization.

"When these pillars are aligned, nonprofits not only secure the financial resources they need. But also build a community of like-minded, principled individuals," Streiff continues. "Embrace these three principles as the bedrock of your fundraising strategy, and watch as your nonprofit thrives, creating lasting change in the lives of those you serve."

So as you begin to cultivate donors, you'll learn in this chapter about five mindsets to change: **the best fundraiser (the CEO), serving and raising at the same time, fundraising isn't for the proud, you are the prize,** and a reminder to **reframe *no* as redirection.**

## CEO: Chief Earning Officer.

The first mindset we'll cover is whose job it is to cultivate donors in the first place. No doubt: a founder or CEO is always the best fundraiser.

After working with 340 nonprofit organizations in 51 countries (and running a nonprofit hybrid myself) this truth holds without exception. We've seen it repeatedly with clients. From Nafisa at Wajamama to George at Building Tomorrow to Richa and Vedant at Labhya — top leaders are top rainmakers.

So, here's some straight talk for all those leaders who disdain the money side of things. Many of you started as doctors, lawyers, teachers, engineers, and other incredible specialties. However, if you secretly despise fundraising, funding will elude you. If you loathe raising money, money will fail you.[1] If you dislike storytelling, stories will neglect you. And if you resent brand building, awareness will avoid you.

That's why many of you try to delegate fundraising — spending your time instead on programs, products, operations, and countless other priorities.

But funders — especially high-net-worths — want *you*. You own the brand. You are the best at storytelling. You are responsible for fundraising.

Yes, your development and comms team should help you with the tactics. Yes, it may only require 50% of your time, such as focusing on high-value donors. And yes, you can hire a consultant to find leads and guide the process.

However, working *on* vs. *in* the business[2] is what leaders do. You're the cash catalyst. The funding flame. The gold getter.

So embrace funding, or it will elude you.

Lead. Fund. Repeat.

> *"Most CEOs would rather have a root canal than make a solicitation call on a wealthy prospect. If you're not willing to raise money, you shouldn't be in the CEO position. It's part and parcel of the job." — Nonprofit World*

That's precisely why all you leaders can't just focus on the work. And can't keep treating fundraising like a separate function, the mindset I'll explain next.

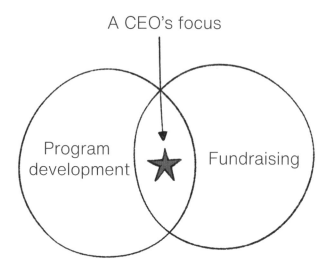

FIGURE 26: A founder or CEO is always the best fundraiser.

## Serve to raise: raise to serve.

The second donor cultivation mindset is to remember that most nonprofits unknowingly run two businesses at once.

**One to serve communities.**

**Another to raise money.**

But you don't properly acquire and cultivate donors by keeping them separate. So, build a brand that includes both.

Name the people you serve — participants, beneficiaries, or whatever you may call them — in your theory of change (remember Chapter 1). Then target your priority audiences (Chapter 8) — often mostly funders — in your positioning strategy and marketing communications.

Then integrate both sides of the organization in your strategic plan. This is a more challenging step than in the private sector, where customers are also payers. But without one or the other value proposition, the brand is incomplete.

> *"It's the muted market. In one direction we offer our theory of change (products, services) to the communities we serve. And in the other direction we offer insight, impact data, and inspiration to those who would fund the work. We have to understand the motivations and dynamics driving both sets of customers to hit that sweet spot where needs on both sides of the equation are consistently met." — Sebastian Africano, nonprofit leader and teacher (United States)*

Dual focus, singular success. Harmonize efforts. Heighten outcomes.

## Fundraising is not for the proud.

The third cultivation mindset to change is that most donors don't care as much as you do — about all the little details of your work. So stop trying to sound sophisticated.

Instead, remember "fundraising is not for the proud," says fundraising expert Jeff Brooks.[3] "It's not for those who need to demonstrate their expertise and who think everyone else should be just as interested in their field as they are."

He continues with a telling example, for those nonprofits that work to alleviate hunger:

"One of the great fundraising offers is the $1.79 meal. It's a great offer because it's specific, it's something that's in the life experience of your donor — and it's cheap."

Many nonprofits that could utilize this simple fundraising message do much more than serve meals, Brooks says.

"But donors want solid, simple, clear offers they can understand. Are you willing to say, 'Sorry, Ms. Donor. We don't want your money until you comprehend our programs in all their complex fullness.'"

"That's an expensive attitude," he adds. "It's one some nonprofits take."

The only exception I'll make here is when dealing with savvy trusts and foundations that often expect rigorous details. For example, with our client Food for Education, we couldn't just focus the brand on school meals. We also messaged their blueprint for scale with African governments.

Otherwise, don't forget these wise words from the book *Made to Stick*. "People are tempted to tell you everything, with perfect accuracy, right up front, when they should be giving you just enough info to be useful, then a little more, then a little more."

And this reminder from the positioning strategy expert April Dunford who says, "It's always better to be a little boring than completely baffling."

Pride complicates. Clarity converts.

Don't impress. Inspire.

# You are the prize: the donor isn't.

When cultivating donors, here's a fourth mindset to change.

**Reject:** "We won a new grant."

**Embrace:** "They won a new grantee."

**Or better yet:** "We both won a new partnership."

To shift this mindset, stop building your brand with a *handout* for the funder's money. And start fundraising like it's a *handshake* between equals.

> *"Nonprofits need the funds, but the donor also needs results and impact. It's a win/win situation for all."*
> — *Mickness Aeschlimann, consultant (Tanzania)*

Here's another take:

"It's not about money," says fundraising program The Eight Principles. "It's about two parties coming together to accomplish something they cannot do alone."

But wait. Aren't we supposed to make the donor the hero?

Rubbish.

That's possibly the worst, most inequitable fundraising advice that suffocates our sector today. Because even we nonprofits aren't the real heroes. We may be the prize in the fundraising relationship, and we may use storytelling techniques to invite the donor into the narrative too.

But it's our communities facing and fighting injustice that are heroic.

Our client, Muso, is a great example of this mindset. Check out the Funder Practices for Transformative Partnership on their website. *They* as the nonprofit say what *they* expect from donors before accepting money.

CEO Ari Johnson sums it up: "We need to move away from transactional relationships and toward partnerships. Part of that is doing mutual diligence, finding a good match, and then striving together to be worthy of those we serve."

So flip the script. Rewrite the narrative. Your marketing will be bolder. Your community will be centered. You'll attract greater funder attention. Conversations will become more just. And we can perhaps shift the doer-donor power imbalance once and for all.

You are the prize. Prizes don't chase. And stars don't audition.

## *No* isn't rejection: it's redirection.

One more mindset on cultivation before we get into donor solicitation in Chapter 18. *No* is a weapon. You might hate to hear it and say it. But that's a no-torious fundraising issue.

Because hearing a hesitant *maybe* from a donor can be far more damaging than a clear *no*. And you saying *no* to the wrong fundraising opportunities can boost credibility and attract better funders the next time around.

## Hearing *no.*

"*No* is the second-best answer we can hear," says the sales training firm Win Without Pitching. "It is far preferable to *maybe* or *we'll get back to you* or to silence."

(I personally remember an early — and exciting! — fundraising *maybe* from a Big Bang Philanthropy foundation that turned into silence. In the months it took me to chase down the eventual *no*, the ambiguity demoralized and distracted our team.)

Rejection is redirection. So think of *no* as a beginning, not an end. It signals either a pivot point or a chance to step away clean.

> "*No* is a bridge to an ongoing relationship. *No* gives us some clues as to where that person is in their decision-making process and whether *no* is rooted in a timing issue, a pricing issue, or a misalignment of vision and values."
> — Tania Bhattacharyya, fundraiser (United States)

## Saying *no.*

"An unfortunate but indisputable trait of humans is how profoundly we are repulsed by neediness," continues Win Without Pitching. "We push others away and lose their respect by always saying *yes*, by reeking of *yes*."

That's why this is a powerful piece of brand messaging when making an ask:

**Feel free to say no...**

And that's why fundraising consultant Jeff Brooks advises giving donors permission not to donate. "It's not some kind of sneaky mind-control," he says. "And it's not going to double or triple your response rates. But it can help some donors take your offer just a bit more seriously."

Although it's actually a two-way street.

"It isn't easy for organizations desperately or even existentially in need of funding to say no to a funder," remarks foundation trustee Richard Marker. "But a healthy relationship should allow and a responsible nonprofit needs to be able to say no in some circumstances, and *no* should be respected by the funder."

So remember this *no*-tion:

*Maybe* is the real enemy.

*No* strengthens resolve.

*No* cultivates respect.

*No* boosts credibility.

*No* ignites potential.

*No* is not failure.

*No* builds trust.

*No* is clarity.

Leverage it. Enforce it. Own it.

And owning it comes in your donor solicitation stage, up next in Chapter 18. Let's carry on.

# Summary.

1. Even an expert fundraiser admitted that the first step in fundraising isn't identification or qualification or even cultivation — it's brand awareness.

2. In early- and growth-stage nonprofits, the single best donor cultivator (and fundraiser!) is one of the founders and/or the CEO. If you secretly loathe money, it will elude you.

3. In order to improve donor cultivation, nonprofits must not silo the two sides of the business — which typically means having one side to serve communities and another to raise money.

4. Don't get too proud in your fundraising and forget to simplify the donor offer. Inspire, don't impress.

5. Stop building your brand by holding a hand out for the funder's money. And start fundraising as if it's a handshake between equals.

6. *No* isn't rejection. It's redirection. So as you begin soliciting donors, remember that a clear redirection is much better than an unclear *maybe* — or even the dreaded silence.

# 18. SOLICITATION

## You can't wake a donor who is pretending to be asleep.

The Navajo are a Native American people known for abundant ancient wisdom. And this Navajo proverb might strike a chord for your fundraising:

**You can't wake a person who is pretending to be asleep.**

That's why I say, when it comes to solicitation, ignore the donors who ignore you. Move on.

Because there's a key for every lock. And a donor for every nonprofit. Quit soliciting.

> *"Unresponsive isn't just not interested, it's not ready. Time is precious. Invest your energy in those who actively engage, who show genuine interest."* — Jesse Bilege, analyst (Tanzania)

There's no marketing collateral, fundraising campaign, or relentless persistence that will make someone care in the first place if they're purposefully ignoring you.

Here's why this matters: prospects can smell desperation. So, "The more you constantly chase to create an opportunity, the less likely you are to create an opportunity," says marketing leader Scott Cantrell. "And the more likely they are to become annoyed, or angry, or just not respond at all."

Don't get me wrong. You can possibly awaken an audience that was *once* engaged. Even so, the recapture rate of lapsed donors is just 4% — if they stop giving, the chances of their ever donating again are minimal.[1]

When do you move on? Here are the top five signs it's time to stop chasing a prospect, from sales expert Liz Wendling.

- They're not open to sharing information.

- They're not returning your calls and emails.

- They're not willing to set up another meeting.

- They won't ask/answer tough questions.

- They're not happy to see you.

"Stop calling, stop emailing, stop begging for one more meeting, and stop acting desperate. Dump them and move on," Wendling advises. "Instead of chasing prospects who don't want to be caught, invest your time in prospects who engage with you instead of run from you."

So, with solicitation as this chapter's focus (*the ask!*), you'll learn a number of mindsets to change: **the five stages of donors, social proof, the right story, listening to donors,** and **proposal writing.**

# The five stages of donors.

The first donor solicitation mindset is to figure out the stage of the donor. *Before* the ask.

I know I've been preaching in this book the power of message consistency. But once you nail down your core, consistent messaging — there's an important nuance to consider.

Your prospects are at different stages of awareness. And not every donor knows the same thing about a social problem, the potential solutions, or your brand.

For example, using industry jargon with a new individual donor will make them feel lost. Or, telling too many participant stories to a foundation that is ready to give will make them impatient.

So use this five-stage awareness cycle in Figure 27 to tailor your next conversation or marketing message.

| | DONOR STAGE | BEST MESSAGING |
|---|---|---|
| 1 | **Unaware:** aren't yet aware of the social problem you solve | Use storytelling, data & educational content about the issue (not your work) |
| 2 | **Problem aware:** understand the problem, but not potential solutions | Agitate the pain points & share outcomes & benefits of solving the problem |
| 3 | **Solution aware:** get the solution, but don't realize your org provides it | Introduce your mission, your intervention & exactly the way it works |
| 4 | **Organization aware:** know your solution, but not sure they want to fund | Provide impact data for proof, participant testimonials & why you're unique |
| 5 | **Most aware:** want to fund you — just need to know when & how much | Keep messaging concise, make the ask & explain how their gift will be used |

FIGURE 27: The five stages of donors, adapted from Eugene Schwartz.[2]

Just think: the next time you're going into a fundraising conversation or writing some marketing copy, *where is this prospect in their awareness cycle?*

Then deliver the right messaging to them. Your goal is to move donors to the next level of understanding. And guess what? If you introduce information in this proper sequence, a prospect can fly through these stages quickly — sometimes even in the same conversation.

## Social proof: don't tell funders how awesome you are.

Once you figure out the stage of the donor, here's another solicitation mindset to change: it doesn't work to tell funders how great we are. We all say we're awesome. Instead, nonprofits can use a subtle (but mighty!) psychological hack in solicitation communications:

Social proof.

Otherwise known as *herd mentality* or the *imitation effect*. From cave paintings to TikTok trends, our yearning to echo the tribe is hardwired. And using social proof in your fundraising, sales, and brand communications isn't just effective — it's evolutionary magic.

Because "the greater the number of people who find any idea correct, the more the idea will be correct," according to the groundbreaking book *Influence: The Psychology of Persuasion*.

Some 95% of people are imitators and only 5% are initiators, according to the book's research. So for brand builders, our audiences are persuaded more by the actions of others than by any other proof we can offer.

> *"Even someone inclined to support your cause may not give unless you push the right buttons. Of all the ways to do that, social proof is among the easiest and most successful. When you say your organization rocks, who really believes you? When someone else says the same thing, that's another ballgame entirely. Their independent seal of approval acts as a decision-making shortcut, helping resolve any doubts your organization is top notch and worthy of investment."* — Claire Axelrad, J.D., CFRE, fundraising expert (United States)[3]

So how can you use social proof in your brand and donor solicitations?

- Case studies to show instead of tell

- Awards/recognitions you've received

- Beneficiary and customer impact stories

- Donor logos in your fundraising materials

- Name dropping when speaking with funders

- Reviews like GuideStar or Charity Navigator

- Fundraising events hosted by existing donors

- Articles and media mentions about your work

- Quotes and testimonials that sing your praises

To see a real-world client example, we used social proof — a lot! — in our brand work for Community Health Impact Coalition. As a nonprofit coalition with countless members, allies, funders, government partners, and community health workers — you'll see dozens of logos and well-known names scattered throughout their website and fundraising materials. One glance at their brand and they *feel* legit, before you read a single line.

And speaking of the power of quotes, see below. In all the promotions for our Mighty Ally online course, we feature testimonials from nonprofit leaders who have completed it. Like:

> *"I have been working for NGOs for over five years now, and have never had such an 'ah-ha' moment as I have had ✦ multiple times ✦ throughout this course. AND, I am only halfway through." — Michaela Higgins Sørensen, communications director (Denmark)*

See how much more effective that is than if you saw an advertisement trying to sell you on our course? I proved my point, now prove yours. Social proof worked here, so make it work for you.

## Three stories: rally, don't just relay.

Now that you've thought about the donor stage and how to incorporate social proof into your solicitation, the next mindset to change is that your fundraising ask might be telling the wrong story. Because there are three types of brand stories, but only one converts donors. Here's the breakdown:

### The participant story.

Your donor appeals often describe one participant who you've helped. And you urge funders to contribute. While suitable for newsletters or annual reports, these past-tense narratives typically don't excel in fundraising.

### The organizational story.

Your fundraising content can also concentrate on the organization's mission, its leaders, awards won, and values. This messaging may interest insiders (like board members), but it's dull to most audiences and raises even less money.

### The donation impact story.

Donors are most interested in your future-looking storytelling. Like stories that depict the potential impact of their donations, emphasizing the change that will occur with their gift. Because funders seek assurance that their contribution matters. And by showing them how their gift makes an impact, you find a healthy version of that "make the donor the hero" problem we talked about in Chapter 17.

Fundraising expert Jeff Brooks takes this three-story model a step further. And calls it "two lousy stories and a great one."

"The first two stories at best hint at what their giving might do — and at worst are irrelevant to the donor," he says. "The story about the change that can happen when the donor gets involved raises a lot more funds."

That's why The Better Fundraising Company (which created this model)[4] advises that the best donor solicitation looks like this:

**Right now things are X, but if you give a gift they will be Y.**

A classic before-and-after. Exactly what we did in a holiday campaign for Lwala Community Alliance years ago. We made it clear in their direct mail piece that, "In rural Kenya, 8% of children die before their fifth birthday." However, we quickly told the donation impact story by displaying various options for the donor, such as how $5,000 provides health services for 100 children for one year or $1,000 provides full immunization for 200 kids.

Now keep in mind:

There's of course a time and place to tell the participant and organizational stories. And, naturally, different types of donors need different types of narratives (this model certainly applies more to individuals than to institutional donors).

Yet it still raises this question: are you telling the right story? And if you *are* telling it correctly, don't tell it too much — which is the next solicitation mindset we need to change as a sector.

## Speak as if you're right: listen as if you're wrong.[5]

Soliciting *to* and pitching *at* donors isn't communicating. It's the two-way conversation (speaking *with*) that seals the deal instead of a one-way ask.

So if you're only *telling*, you miss half the solicitation job. To be heard by your donors, teams, and partners, you must listen. Even if you're super-convinced of what your brand is saying. Because "strong opinions, loosely held" is a superpower.

And listening will help you:

- Strengthen relationships

- Uncover hidden needs

- Increase transparency

- Encourage inclusivity

- Anticipate objections

- Identify pain points

- Boost staff morale

- Develop empathy

- Build donor trust

- Enhance clarity

In fact, as the author Jerry Panas says, around 55% of your fundraising meeting should be spent listening.

But "asking for a contribution makes most people nervous, which causes rambling," says storytelling author Lori L. Jacobwith. "And together, we have the perfect storm to make the most common fundraising mistake: talking too much. If you want to get a *yes* — use less words."

The heart of the matter: open ears, open wallets. Dialogue drives donations. And a bit of silence strengthens your voice.

With that two-way conversation in place, you need one final piece of the solicitation puzzle: where and how to actually make the ask. Your proposal.

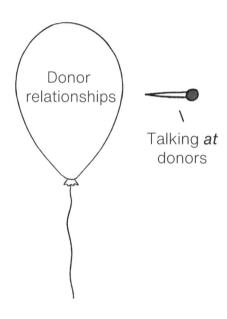

FIGURE 28: Soliciting *to* and pitching *at* donors isn't communicating.

## Pitches intrigue funders: but proposals convince.

A proposal is exactly where you make the ask, so let's change this mindset: a pitch deck is *not* more important. A pitch deck might get much more attention, but it simply starts the conversation. It's your story's opening act. The finale of your donor solicitation is a proposal. So a proposal or grant application isn't just paperwork. It's a deal-maker.

For nonprofits submitting a grant application or social enterprises seeking a big sale, a proposal meets the moment when the prospect says *yes* or *no*. You can close many deals without a pitch deck, but rarely without a proposal.

"Although a great proposal by itself seldom wins a deal, a bad proposal can definitely lose one," says author Tom Sant.[6] Make it compelling, or lose the case.

## What is a proposal?

A proposal is a sales tool, not an information packet. It should be the result of numerous discussions with the prospective funder or buyer. Meaning, there should be no surprises — either with money or with the strategy you're suggesting. Instead, it should be seen as a written review of your conversations.

The good news is that proposals can be both effective and easy. There's a formula for them, and best practices do exist. This stuff has long been studied and proven. So it's time to develop your proposal playbook and turn information into persuasion by using the NOSE structure.

**Need:** Show that you understand the key issues or problems faced by your community. Just like other brand materials we've discussed in this book, never lead with your organization. You could also think of this section as *the situation*.

**Outcomes:** Focus on the results that you, your community, your buyer, and/or your funder want to achieve. But don't yet prescribe exact recommendations. This can also be called *the opportunity*.

**Solution:** Highlight the work you do that will deliver the results. You can title this section *products and programs*. And include the budget options, if applicable.

**Evidence:** Provide proof that you can deliver that solution. Some proposals call this section *our model*. Include your experience, case studies, impact, and/or testimonials.

> *"Focus on their pain to get their attention. Focus on their gain to get their commitment."* — Persuasive Business Proposals

That's it. Four sections to a proposal, and a page per section is plenty. Nobody has time to read 30 pages. It's better to send 1–2 pages of targeted text than to scramble together countless pages of general blah-blah.

Per Sant's survey of thousands of proposal evaluators, the number one answer to what they hate is "proposals that are too wordy." In a real-world experiment with a table full of documents, every evaluator first reached for the smallest proposal.

These proposal best practices should help you land more money, for sure. But it's not just *new* money that matters (it's keeping that money as well).

That's why it's time to switch to the other side of the coin: attitudes for donor retention, coming up in the next section.

# Summary.

1. Ignore the donors who ignore you. Quit soliciting, because there's a key for every lock and a donor for every nonprofit.

2. When soliciting donors, remember to reject the proud boast, "We won a new grant" and instead embrace, "They won a new grantee."

3. Social proof — like testimonials, other donor logos, awards won, and so on — is more valuable than telling a donor yourself how awesome you are.

4. There are three types of donor stories (participant, organizational, and donor impact) — but the latter is best at raising money.

5. Nonprofit leaders often place too much importance on top-of-the-funnel communications assets like pitch decks, when in reality a proposal is the deal-maker.

# DONOR RETENTION
## Manage and maintain your existing donors and resources with these brand attitudes.

For years, an image has gone viral around many social media platforms. "Think like a farmer," it says, with classic advice such as "don't blame the crop for not growing fast enough" and "choose the best plants for the soil."

That viral post constantly reminds me that fundraising is mostly about farming, not hunting. Because there are five ways to raise more money:

Find new donors (*hunting*).

Retain existing donors (*farming*).

Increase average gift size (*farming*).

Get donors to give more often (*farming*).

Grow word-of-mouth donor referrals (*farming*).

Only those five. And farming requires consistency. Being *consistently average* with existing donors will raise more money than if your brand is *inconsistently brilliant* with new ones.

Just think about the power of compounding interest in finance. Or that among the world's 15 largest nonprofits, all were founded before 1979.[1]

Unfortunately, most poverty and injustice will take a lifetime to solve. So we need your fundraising resilience. We need your donors to stick around for a long time. It's a marathon, not a sprint. And consistency wins the fundraising race.

*"A little rain each day will fill the rivers to overflowing."*
*— African proverb*

As we move from ways to acquire your donors to ways to keep them, in this section you'll learn more about donor retention: **hunting vs. farming** and **growing donors, not just donations.** Then we'll look at two parts of donor retention in Chapters 19 and 20.

## Donor farming: beats donor hunting.

Donor hunting is expensive. Funder farming is cheaper. Hunting involves a lot of luck. Farming is mostly within your control. Hunting is difficult, since every nonprofit is attempting it. Farming is easier, because many leaders ignore it. Hunting has fewer proven formulas. Farming flourishes through relationships and brand strategy.

This is why brand loyalty plants the seeds for maximized funding.

*"Non-fundraisers tend to assume the only way to grow income is to add new donors to your donor pool. So there is a tendency at the board and senior leadership level to put too much focus on the new." — Michelle Benson, philanthropy advisor (England)*

The reality is that charities are more likely to get new money from warm existing donors than cold new ones, according to Benson.

"The second assumption is *once a donor, always a donor*. As if people donate and then automatically stick around," she remarks. "Of course this is not true — fundraisers know good stewardship sows the seed to the next donation."

Her final advice?

Charities have to spark a relationship (and brand) with a new prospect and must earn their trust to get a donation. So neglecting that relationship (and brand) once a donation has been made is how you:

- Waste all your previous efforts.

- Generate a terrible reputation among donors.

- Stall out instead of advancing income with a solid retention plan.

- Miss the opportunity to grow new income from trading up existing donors.

"Good stewardship also leads to the greatest fundraising prize of all — donor askers or word-of-mouth among a look-alike audience you want to attract," Benson concludes. "When your donors start to fundraise for you, your reach and endorsements increase while your costs decrease."

The root of success here: you only have five ways to raise more money, and four of them require farming, not hunting.

Less snare, more sow. Less chase, more cultivate.

# Grow donors: not just donations.

You don't need new funders. Not until you've maximized the ones you have. And not until you've regained a lot of your lapsed donors.

Because donor retention beats donor acquisition.

All day, every day.

Retention over acquisition is a well-known, well-practiced path to private-sector brand growth. Yet the nonprofit starvation cycle causes leaders to chase more, more, more... new, new, new... better, better, better.

So let's talk about these vital fundraising data:[2]

- Nearly seven out of 10 donors will give once, and never again.

- Every $100 gained is offset by $96 in losses through donor attrition.

- Most major gifts are made after 18–24 touchpoints and five years of smaller giving.

- The cost to continually acquire new donors runs 50–100% more than the dollars collected.

- The recapture rate of lapsed donors is just 5% — so if they stop giving, the chances of their ever giving again are minimal.

*"Although acquisition of new donors is important, the numbers don't lie. The value proposition and financial benefit for your organization fall clearly on keeping the donors you have over finding new donors." — Amy Eisenstein, fundraising writer (United States)*

Then what is the solution to keep and grow existing funders?

Create a priority audience — just for them.

Generate value propositions — just for them.

Develop a positioning strategy — just for them.

Execute a communications plan — just for them.

Understand the fundraising data — just for them.

In other words: create a brand strategy — just for them. And that's precisely what Mighty Ally did with client Nyaka, after realizing that 48% of givers were dropping off each year. Their retention rate was better than the industry average. But our new brand strategy for existing donors still led to an additional $350,000 in donations for Nyaka within 12 months.

So there's no need to hunt for diamonds. Sometimes, you're standing on the mine.

How do you better steward donors in that mine? For one thing: stop thinking that stewardship is different from donor communications — the topic of Chapter 19, coming at you next.

# Summary.

1. Fundraising is mostly farming, not hunting. Because there are only five ways to raise more money, and four of them are donor retention (meaning, farming).

2. Nonprofits are more likely to get new money from warm existing donors than cold distant ones.

3. You don't need new funders. Not until you've maximized the ones you have. And not until you've regained as many of your lapsed donors as possible.

4. Retention over acquisition is a well-known goal in the private sector. Yet the nonprofit starvation cycle causes leaders to chase more, more, more, new, new, new.

5. The solution to keep and then grow your existing funders: brand strategy.

# 19. STEWARDSHIP
## Stop stewarding, start communicating.

Donor stewardship isn't working.

Stewardship is one of the classic sections of the old-school fundraising cycle, back in Figure 25. And according to Bloomerang, it's "a long-term strategy to strengthen those relationships in the hopes of earning repeat donations."

But just look at our sector's dismal donor retention rates, discussed in the previous chapter. This collective weakness around retaining donors is why I propose that the term *stewardship* should be rebranded — as donor *communications*.

Because there really isn't any other way to steward a donor than to communicate with them via digital, print, on-air, or in-person channels. But many nonprofit leaders think stewardship is the sole responsibility of the fundraising team. In reality, it belongs to everyone responsible for the brand. Hint: that's anyone in the organization with a mouth or a keyboard.

This mismatched terminology could explain why donor stewardship is often done so poorly. Or not at all. Like the two main reasons donors don't give again:[1]

They weren't told how their first gift was used.

They didn't feel thanked.

Ouch. That's just basic communications.

And that's why author Kay Sprinkel Grace says the real work begins *after* you receive the gift. "This is the most important, yet most neglected piece of the fundraising process," she advises.

In this chapter, you'll learn how to better steward donors and resources with these brand attitudes: **the rule of seven, turning data into stories, communicating your budget well, educating donors about overhead,** and **the power of repetition.**

## The rule of seven: touchpoints and thank-yous.

So how might you do donor stewardship better? Strong fundraising hinges on strong donor relationships, and central to these relationships are strong communications. So remember the rule of seven. For each funding request, balance it with at least seven engaging brand touchpoints.

Some examples:

- Email surveys

- Program tours

- Video updates

- Thank-you calls

- Thank-you notes

- Email newsletters

- In-person meetings

- Social media tagging

- Milestone celebrations

- Asking for advice/input

- Annual report mentions

- Behind-the-scenes peeks

- Text and WhatsApp messages

- Invitations to events or webinars

- Gift confirmations and tax receipts

- Handwritten holiday or birthday cards

- Impact update (how the gift was used)

In other words, engage the donor seven times with your communications plan — over the course of the next year — before you even think about fundraising again.

I mentioned our client Nyaka in the donor retention section and how we boosted repeat giving. Some of our tactics simply followed this rule of seven. Like ensuring the online donation tax receipt included a personal thank you letter, prompting the founder to personally contact major givers, and adding all donors to the email list so they could see the impact via the newsletters. Easy stuff, easy communications, but often overlooked.

That's how you achieve less attrition, more attention.

# Data: summaries of thousands of stories.

Stewardship starts with a story. Yet sometimes nonprofit leaders think the best way to show good stewardship of funds is to overly report on the facts. To invest more in monitoring and evaluation and to make sure donors see the data.

But here are four insights for your impact data and fundraising:

- An M&E report (itself) doesn't land you funding.

- Everyone is claiming "evidence based" these days.

- Testimonials often outperform other forms of measurement.

- You can't keep donors with a randomized control trial (RCT) alone.

Because "data are just summaries of thousands of stories," says the book *Made to Stick*. Telling a few of those stories is what makes the data stick.

We've seen nonprofit clients with a sexy RCT that were far from fundable. Some of them boasting an "evidence base" of "proven impact" didn't even have a clear theory of change.

So their brand and fundraising fell flat.

On the other hand, many clients don't have RCTs or fancy monitoring and evaluation — yet raise millions of dollars.

Nobody has figured out how to solve poverty and injustice. So foundations and donors mostly place bets on leaders, their ideas, healthy organizations, and signs of progress. They don't invest because of your perfect impact data.

Storytelling is how you communicate a better world that doesn't exist yet. Then you invite funders into it (think back to the vision element of Chapter 3). Sure, impact data can significantly boost donor retention — after the storytelling honeymoon has ended. And sure, impact data certainly matters more for stewardship as you scale beyond the growth stage. Especially for big aid funding.

But many of you are still just trying to find sustainability. To get out of the nonprofit starvation cycle. So I'd say:

Of course, measure your work. Of course, establish solid M&E systems. Of course, communicate the metrics (both good and bad).

But remember that data is the condensed version of countless narratives. You must share those stories to give the numbers life. Just as I showed you in Chapter 18, you have three types of stories to use, and the donation impact story converts best.

Don't just count numbers; make the numbers count.

Numbers tell        Stories sell

FIGURE 29: Data are just summaries of thousands of stories.

# A budget: a story in numbers.

Speaking of the numbers, budgets help you raise money — not just spend it. Financials are part of your messaging too. And budgeting is part of a good donor stewardship strategy.

Because "a well-communicated budget is a fundraising tool," says our client Robin Bruce at Dovetail Impact Foundation.

And every donor wants to see how their money was used. That's why our Mighty Ally brand training for Dovetail grantees includes an ally who delivers a communicating budgets module.

So, nonprofit leaders — don't fully delegate this important fundraising tool to your finance team. And don't ask them to create a budget in a silo. (Yes, this means those of us CEOs who loathe accounting.)

Instead, work together to integrate these budgeting ideas:

**Align the budget with your theory of change:** Talk about how your expenses are necessary for the mission and vision your donors have invested in.

**Showcase transparency in your budget:** Openly share your budget allocation to build trust and demonstrate effective use of funds.

**Connect budgets to success stories:** Link budget elements to successful outcomes to make the financial narrative both compelling and relatable.

**Turn budget challenges into appeals:** Be honest. Candidly share budget constraints that motivate donors to contribute toward overcoming these shortfalls.

**Use budget comparisons for impact:** Compare past and present budgets to demonstrate growth, development, and increased impact over time.

**Design visuals for budget line items:** Employ visual aids like graphs and infographics to make complex financial data more accessible and engaging.

The central idea here:

A budget is a moral document.[2] Meaning, "it tells us, mathematically, what areas, issues, things, or people are most important to the creators of that budget, and which are least important," says preacher and justice advocate Jim Wallis.

So dare to think about budgeting differently. It isn't just numbers. It's a narrative. Make every line item a character in your story.

# Low overhead: it can't make a lousy charity good.

Here's a line item that needs more attention in all our stories. And here's another main area we get wrong in our donor stewardship and fundraising communications: overhead.

We either fall victim to the myth, not wanting to lose the donor if we communicate overhead percentages that are too high (thinking that we're not stewarding "their" funding well). Or we pretend during our donor stewardship conversations that nonprofits aren't like every other business on earth that needs investment. Or maybe we dance around the topic altogether.

It's long past time to take the bull by the horns. So how do we talk to donors about overhead? Repeat after me:

Overhead is fuel. Not fluff.

Overhead is a virtue. Not a vice.

Overhead is pivotal. Not peripheral.

Overhead is operational. Not optional.

Overhead is investment. Not indulgence.

> *"You can't make a lousy charity good by having a low overhead." — Will MacAskill, effective altruism philosopher (Scotland)*

But the *right* overhead *can* make "a lousy charity good." So here are 35 essentials worth investing in:

| OBVIOUS ESSENTIALS | NOT-SO-OBVIOUS ESSENTIALS |
| --- | --- |
| Utilities | Brand |
| Salaries | Mental health |
| Technology | Staff retention |
| Fundraising | Theory of change |
| Recruitment | Risk management |
| Infrastructure | Strategic planning |
| Legal consultation | Employee benefits |
| Equipment & supplies | Contingency funds |
| Leadership & staff training | Positioning strategy |
| Board development & governance | Succession planning |
| | Organizational culture |
| | Advocacy & lobbying |
| | Stakeholder convenings |
| | Innovation & research |
| | Team-building activities |
| | Monitoring & evaluation |
| | Marketing communications |
| | Diversity, equity & inclusion |
| | Financial management systems |
| | Partnerships & collaborations |
| | Intellectual property protection |
| | Ethical standards & compliance |

FIGURE 30: Overhead essentials.

These critical factors in nonprofit performance continue to be underfunded, or deprioritized, or even considered inessential bloat. Nonprofits actually lose out on money when categorizing some of these overhead items as inessential, "indirect costs."

"What's more important is the practice of considering whether an expense advances your impact," says fundraiser Jenna Rogers-Rafferty. "If you can justify that it does with a straight face to your funder, you should consider it a direct cost and feel empowered to defend that decision."

But the issue is way bigger than skillful budgeting.

> *"The focus on overhead is no longer just annoying, it's perpetuating inequity and injustice." — Vu Le, blogger and speaker (United States)[3]*

Unlike some social justice challenges we're fighting — with no known solutions yet — the overhead myth is a positioning and storytelling problem. In other words, it's an opportunity to rebrand overhead. Sadly, says Le, nonprofits are one of the biggest drivers of this narrative. He continues:

> *"It's time for a change. Stop furthering the idea that 'overhead' is bad. Operating, administrative, and fundraising expenses are necessary for us to do effective work."*

I personally think that the "giving 100% to the cause" pitch is the worst offender. It's a short-term win, true, but a long-term loss — for you *and* the sector. Although foundations must evolve too.

"If you are restricting funding and focusing on overhead, you are actively preventing nonprofits from doing their work," Le concludes. "You are helping to spread the fires of injustice."

Let's shift the narrative. Because myths hold power only if we let them. One of the best ways to change language and improve mindsets? Repeat, repeat, repeat.

## Repetition: say it again for all the funders in the back.

If enough donors say it about you, it's true. And funders trust familiar organizations. But they don't trust unfamiliar brands. What's the lesson here for donor stewardship? The power of repetition.

Let me explain.

The Chinese proverb "Three Men Make a Tiger" says that people will believe anything if enough others tell them it's true (just three other people, in fact). Like a tiger roaming around the village at night.

Nobel Prize-winning psychologist Daniel Kahneman explains something similar:

> *"A reliable way to make people believe... is frequent repetition, because familiarity is not easily distinguished from truth."*

How does it work?

It's called the *mere-exposure effect*. It's a psychological phenomenon. We all eventually trust, believe, and prefer things for no other reason than because we've heard about them enough times. And once a donor trusts, believes, and prefers your nonprofit — you retain their gift.

So use this effect in your donor retention strategies:

**Keep your messaging consistent.**

**Repeat it on each and every comms channel.**

Sometimes the formula isn't complicated. And if repetition alone makes people believe in a phony tiger (or a corrupt politician, ahem), surely our nonprofits can capitalize on this phenomenon with our donor storytelling.

In short: let familiarity fuel your funding. Brand consistency = credibility. Repeat, repeat, repeat to resonate and retain donors.

Also repeat, repeat, repeat this important message that's rarely discussed: diversified funding is a nonprofit nemesis.

*Blasphemy*, you say! But before you argue, let's dig into the facts in Chapter 20.

# Summary.

1. Nonprofit leaders should stop thinking of donor stewardship as a separate endeavor owned by fundraising. It's simply donor communications, and everyone owns it.

2. After you receive a donor gift, what you do next is "the most important, yet most neglected piece of the fundraising process," according to Kay Sprinkel Grace.

3. One of the best ways to steward and retain a donor is through the power of repetition: keep your message consistent, and repeat it on each and every comms channel.

4. Of all the messages that need repeating in our sector, the right overhead *can* make "a lousy charity good."

5. Budgeting is just a story in numbers — and should be part of your donor retention strategy, because every donor wants to know how their money was spent.

# 20. ENGAGEMENT

Diversified funding is a nonprofit nemesis.

Here's a hard truth nobody is talking about:

Diversified fundraising helps you survive early on. But it's not how you get really big, and it's nearly impossible to engage (well) with multiple types of funders at once.

Nonprofit CEO Jamie Bearse says that your board members might believe "raising money is like investing in the stock market — a balanced portfolio will ultimately lead to financial success."[1]

Your board members are dead wrong.

So when it comes to retaining and engaging funders, we'll start this chapter by busting **the donor diversification myth.** Then you'll learn the difference between **partner vs. grantee engagement** and **how you can engage foundation brands.**

Let this sink in.

Of those unicorn nonprofits that reach $50 million in annual budget, 90% of them raised the bulk of it from a single type (or category) of funding. Such as individual donors, foundations, corporations, government, *or* service fees. Not by accumulating various types of funding.

To be clear, I'm not talking about relying on a single donor. That's too risky. Instead, I'm saying you must engage and grow a single *type* of donor, of which many different donors in that category are funding you. That's how you get big.

The Bridgespan Group found this secret formula in a study of 200,000 nonprofits over 40 years. They call it *The Myth of Diversification*.[2] And their evidence contradicts a lot of conventional but inaccurate wisdom in our sector.

All that said, Bearse explains that most nonprofits — egged on by board members and consultants — try to grow through diversification and ignore their limits. Nonprofits have a limited understanding of all the donor types, limited time to learn from trial and error, and limited resources to take full advantage of any one type — much less many.

> *"Small- and mid-sized nonprofits seeking to grow can benefit from identifying a primary funding source early in their life cycle, which can be aligned with their program model. Most nonprofits do not seek to get really big. Still, even for those that seek to sustain themselves at a smaller scale, it may be important to focus on one or two main revenue categories and build the capabilities needed to achieve that focus."* — The Bridgespan Group

In other words: if you want to grow significantly, you have to eventually muster the courage to put all your fundraising eggs into one basket. And engage all those eggs in that one basket. As Bearse explains, engaging around a single donor type works well because:

- It provides clarity and efficiency.

- It gives you better resource allocation.

- It offers you more scalability and predictability.

- It affords you new opportunities and ideas for innovation.

- And (the topic of this book) it allows you to build a strong brand identity.

A lot of our clients take this approach. Community Partners International went from $5 million in budget to more than $55 million within a few years, mostly from big aid government grants. And Education Development Trust grew to more than $100 million in size, mostly from service fees for its consultancy work.

Ready to take it a step further? Below are the most common funding types of big nonprofits with budgets of $50 million or more:

- 40% of them get the most funding from **government grants.**

- **Program services/earned revenue** and **corporate donations** are the next most prevalent funding types.

- While only 12% of big nonprofits get the bulk from **foundations and individuals,** this is the fastest-growing source.

- Only 3% of big nonprofits rely on **small gifts** of under $10,000 as the leading source of income.

*"Each funding source is its own business model. No org can simultaneously run five business models at once. Boards can pressure leaders to pursue diversification. I would ask Boards to encourage the right kind of diversification: more funders in a primary source."* —
*Jane Leu, fundraising expert and social entrepreneur (Philippines)*

So why aren't more nonprofit brands better focused in their funding? Fear.

In the early years, reaching $500,000 or even $5 million in size requires being scrappy and taking whatever you can get. Doing what it takes to stay alive.

But to break through the valley of death and truly maximize funding? Wave goodbye to traditional diversification beliefs. It's not about casting a wider fundraising net. The data says to be selective in what you're fishing for.

Say *no* to say *yes*. Because mastery in fundraising focus = mastery in engagement.

*"When nonprofits are small, they often raise money from a wide variety of sources. That's because there are many potential donors who are able to give small amounts of money, and because a particularly inspiring executive director can stand out from the crowd and convince these small donors to give. But when very large sums of money are involved, the picture changes."* —
*The Bridgespan Group*

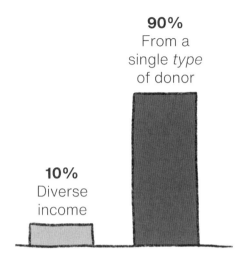

FIGURE 31: The myth of diversified funding.

## Partners collaborate: not dictate.

Let's talk about another reason that donor engagement is so hard for nonprofit leaders. Many funders claim to be *partners* with the nonprofits they support. But in truth, many of us nonprofit leaders are made to feel like *grantees*.

So, nonprofits: if you're being told you're a partner but aren't being engaged like one — you can seek hassle-free, unrestricted money and just call it gifts. You don't have to continue the charade and pretend these donors are actually *partners*.

> *"Sometimes the best thing we donors can do to advance social justice is to just write the check and get out of the way." — Vu Le, blogger and speaker (United States)*

This partner vs. grantee language is a messy donor/doer dynamic that leads to a lot of tension, posturing, misaligned expectations, and even damage in our sector. And I wanted to point out this trend to make sure you know you're not alone.

> *"Although foundation language is about shared values and partnerships, foundation behavior (and grantee behavior) reflects the underlying business relationship. Foundations still overwhelmingly make single-year, project grants… exactly how one hires a vendor, and the exact opposite of how one works in a partnership."*
> — *Jan Masaoka, nonprofit leader (United States)*

Jackpot. And data backs it up.

Just 52% of nonprofits believe foundations are even aware of their challenges, according to the Center for Effective Philanthropy.[3] And only a third of nonprofit leaders think funders help them address these challenges.

That's not donor engagement.

I admire the intentions of foundations that list *partners* on their website. Or say "we're in this together." But it's not a partnership for you leaders when a foundation only wires you money and does a field visit every few years. Or when a donor's endowment keeps growing but your nonprofit grant does not. Or when a funder doesn't welcome criticism about its own work.

Maybe that's why most nonprofit leaders we work with don't use the word *partner* about their donors behind closed doors. (Regardless of what they say in public.)

## So what's the harm?

First, pretending to be a partner wastes your fundraising time. Second, imitation partnerships mask our sector's all-too-common donor-driven systems. And third, funders that overly control a "collaboration" can negatively impact the communities we serve.

The book *Unicorns Unite: How Nonprofits & Foundations Can Build Epic Partnerships*[4] offers nonprofit leaders an excellent EPIC Partnerships framework. Think about EPIC when engaging your foundations and creating true partnerships:

**Equally value all inputs,** especially time and money. True partners do not allow any input to eclipse all others in importance, power, or prestige.

**Prioritize the needs of those we serve.** Nonprofits put the needs of clients, communities, and change first. Foundations put the needs of nonprofits and communities first.

**Increase trust and empathy.** Partners identify as peers, trusted colleagues, teammates, and equals who learn from and challenge each other *and* the field to excel.

**Commit to big, bold, and better.** Partners think big, act boldly, and produce better results — through all-in teamwork.

To be clear, I'm 100% for the much-needed balancing of power. But messaging matters. And much of what donors do out there is not real *engagement*. So again, the lesson for you nonprofit leaders is that partnerships should propel, not merely pledge. If that's not on the table with your funders, push them for unrestricted (uninvolved) funds instead.

Or move on.

# How to engage with foundations: allies, not ATMs.

Before we wrap up this donor engagement chapter, it's worth spending time on one specific donor type. One that I told you above was the fastest-growing donor category for big nonprofits. But the one that will also require more of your time and careful orchestration.

Foundations.

It's a donor category that differs greatly from all other funding types, for two reasons.

First, foundations are often more involved in your work than government funders, corporates, high-net-worths, or small givers. As I showed in Figure 25, foundations invest in nonprofits that align with their mission and strategy. (Note: most other donors don't have their own mission and strategy.) That same chart also shows a significant advantage of foundation funding: program officers often have deep knowledge of your topic. (Note: this means they won't usually be passive bystanders.)

The second reason that this funder category is different — and this will get a bit challenging for some people — is because a foundation's money is not theirs.

Gasp.

*"Once a person or a group places their wealth into a foundation, it is no longer theirs. Nobody owns the money in a foundation. It belongs to the foundation, which is also not owned by anybody, not even the founder or the board. The funds in a foundation exist to serve the public good."*
*— Unicorns Unite: How Nonprofits & Foundations Can Build Epic Partnerships (most telling is that a family foundation CEO co-authored this book)*

So a foundation's donations to you are more of a partnership than, let's say, that of a smaller online donor who is truly just giving you their money and trusting you to implement it well. Since it's nobody's money, the two of you (both doer and donor) *should be*, in theory, equally responsible for using it in the name of public good.

So again, you need to learn to engage foundations the right way. Because if you *do* engage them well, Fox Grants shares nine benefits for you:[5]

- Financial support

- Capacity building

- Resource sharing

- Increased visibility

- Community expertise

- Networking opportunities

- Sustainability and stability

- Advocacy and policy influence

- Strategic planning and evaluation

*"By engaging with community and regional foundations, nonprofits can access a wide range of benefits that enhance their capabilities, extend their reach, and deepen their impact within the communities they serve. Building a relationship with a community foundation is similar to nurturing any important relationship: it requires consistency, transparency, mutual respect, and alignment of goals." — Fox Grants*

## Your foundation engagement playbook.

Have I sold you on the fact that you need to better engage and retain your foundation partners? Good. Then consider these five questions to ask foundations (yes, these donor engagement conversations should be a two-way street) in order to engage them in an EPIC Partnership beyond the grant:

- Do they have a theory of change, and can you see a copy?

- Do they also have a strategic plan, and can you see a copy?

- Do they invest in marketing communications for your cause at large?

- Do they go beyond the money to provide post-investment support to grantees like you?

- Do they use their own marketing communications — or funder networks — to promote their other grantees like you?

It shouldn't be scary for you to ask these questions. Undeniably, there are historical and unfair power imbalances at play. But we're all in this together, and philanthropic foundations are changemakers, too. They just have grantmaking as an intervention vs. direct implementation.

Evidence of this point of view is proven in a funder study called Communication Matters. It was published in *Stanford Social Innovation Review* after analyzing hundreds of grantmakers. And here are some takeaways of how foundation engagement can help your nonprofit brand:

- 86% of foundations agree that when they communicate about an issue, it helps their grantees work more boldly.

- Foundations rank as their goals of good communication: build nonprofit comms capacity, build public will, and then influence policy and practice.

- "We can amplify every dollar we spend if the programs we fund find more recognition, more partners, and can influence those who make policies that affect the people we serve," said one foundation leader.

Remember, it's a foundation's responsibility to engage with your brand — beyond just writing you a check. So, push them to do so.

And with this donor engagement chapter complete, your donor lifecycle is complete. This book is almost complete. And your brand is nearing completion, too.

Yet your brand won't be pretty at the beginning. You'll fail a lot, which is the topic of our Conclusion, and the final piece of this book, coming up next.

# Summary.

1. Diversified fundraising is not how you get really big, because 90% of large nonprofits raised the bulk from a single type of funding.

2. It's nearly impossible to engage with multiple donor types at once due to your limited knowledge, limited time, and limited resources.

3. It's hard to maintain true donor engagement when many funders claim to be *partners* with grantees, yet many nonprofits are made to feel only like *grantees*.

4. Foundation engagement should run deeper than other donor types because foundations often have their own mission and strategy, and because their funds exist to serve the public good.

5. Partnering with foundation brands brings you many benefits, so you can ask them direct questions to find the best match for you and always to consider the EPIC Partnerships framework to truly engage beyond the grant.

# CONCLUSION

## Imperfect brands make perfect sense.

Get going, then get good.

As you work to become fundable and findable, you won't start with the perfect brand strategy. Nor are you expected to have the perfect messaging or marketing or pitch deck or website. Even your theory of change is just that — a theory.

Brands are 20% psychology and 20% art. But 60% science.[1] This science means that "some lessons have to be experienced before they can be understood," says investor Michael Batnick.

So get out there. Experiment. And learn from your fundable, findable mistakes. Learn from your data, learn from your donors, then optimize your brand by 1% every day.

Because, as you should know by now, your brand unlocks funding.

Brand unlocks funding

FIGURE 32: The key to fundraising is your brand.

# If you're not embarrassed, you've launched too late.

You now understand why more fundraising itself can't fix your fundraising.

From Chapters 1–6, you learned to *be fundable* — and you now have all the tools you need to create a solid theory of change and strategic plan. From Chapters 7–16, you also learned to *be findable* — I've taught you how to build a robust positioning strategy and marketing communications mix. And thanks to the right mindsets and attitudes around donor acquisition and retention, which we explored in Chapters 17–20, you're ready to *get funding*.

As I promised in the introduction, you now have the understanding and the Fundable/Findable Framework to build a clear, compelling nonprofit brand.

If you turn these ideas into action, you should feel aligned after a few weeks or months of effort. You'll operate with more clarity and confidence, internally. Plus you'll feel amplified — using a louder, sharper voice to reach new audiences and spread big ideas, externally. And in the long term, you'll maximize your funding and advance social justice.

(As an aside — whether or not it's a goal for you and whether or not you admit it — an improved organizational brand will also tremendously help your *own* personal brand as a leader.)

That's your call to arms. You now have more knowledge and advice about building a nonprofit brand than most. And you can do it. Even if you don't feel ready.

I never felt ready.

We landed our first Mighty Ally client back in the day with only a basic black-and-white PowerPoint presentation and the generic code name, *Project X*. And we've been tinkering with our brand ever since. (I cringe at some of our earlier stuff.)

Yet in the laboratory of fundraising and brand management — like in science — the process of theory, mistakes, and learning is never-ending. So as they say in Silicon Valley: if you're not a little embarrassed when it goes live, you've launched too late.[2]

Launch, learn, level up. Trial, tweak, triumph. Hatch, hustle, hone.

> *"Don't wait for perfection. Just start and let the work teach you. No one expects you to get it right in the beginning, and you'll learn more from your mistakes than you will from your early successes anyway. So stop worrying so much and just look at your best bets and go."*
> — *Jacqueline Novogratz, impact investor (United States)*

## Unlike tattoos, most brand mistakes erase.

As you get started — and make some mistakes — it may be helpful to remember that most marketing and donor communications aren't using permanent ink. Consider these imperfections from some of the biggest brands today:

- Apple has failed with more than 20 products.

- Samsung's Note S7 phone caught on fire.

- Toyota recalls millions of cars annually.

- Google Glass lasted only two years.

- Coke bombed with New Coke.

That's why best-selling author James Clear says to think about your decisions in three ways: as hats, haircuts, or tattoos.

## Hats.

Most brand decisions? They're like hats. Try one on, and if it's wrong, no big deal — change it. The cost of these mistakes is low, so experiment often with new brand elements. Like:

- Testing social media formats.

- Aiming to reach a new target audience.

- Picking the best communications channels.

## Haircuts.

Certain brand choices are like haircuts. You can fix the damage, but not without feeling a little awkward for a while. But you should certainly still take these bigger marketing and fundraising risks occasionally. Like:

- Getting assertive in messaging.

- Updating your visual identity system.

- Launching a bold, new advocacy campaign.

Tattoos.

A handful of brand decisions? They're like tattoos. Once they're made, they stick for life — no going back. These brand choices are rare, so it's important to name them, move slowly, and think carefully. Like:

- Firing a chief fundraiser.

- Renaming and rebranding the organization.

- Merging or folding sister brands or sub-brands.

The Golden Rule here? Hats off to making brave fundraising choices, and getting a bold haircut to renew your comms, but you really should ink your brand with intention, not regret.

# To be a noun, do the verb.

As we wrap things up, stop to think about the core premise of this book. Funding is the noun: the result you want. Being fundable and being findable are the verbs: the actions you need to do. So another way of thinking about this encouragement is some leadership advice I wish I had learned earlier:

To be a brand, build your brand.

To be a visionary, cast a vision.

To be an influencer, influence.

To be a storyteller, tell stories.

To be an innovator, innovate.

To be a mobilizer, mobilize.

To be a disruptor, disrupt.

To be a speaker, speak.

To be a leader, lead.

Recognition doesn't come merely from claiming a title. It comes from taking action. Often for a long time before anyone notices. And the same goes for your fundraising.

> *"Let go of the thing that you're trying to be (the noun),*
> *and focus on the actual work you need to be doing (the*
> *verb)."* — *Austin Kleon, artist and author (United States)*

My wedding vows included a similar sentiment — from an admittedly cheesy country music song — saying that love isn't something you're in, it's something you do.[3]

But it took me years to appreciate this leadership advice at work. Actions speak. Titles whisper. Do the verb you wish to be.

## Out of sync? Out of funds.

If you need one final summary for the entire fundable and findable sections of this book, consider the idea of *harmony*. A lack of harmony can crush your fundraising. Your happiness. And brand.

The beautiful quote below popped up in my meditation app one day. Its wise words apply to both life and nonprofit leadership.

*"Happiness is when what you think, what you say, and what you do are in harmony."* — *Mahatma Gandhi, politician and activist (India)*

I can't think of a better definition of brand building. Because:

**What you think** is your theory of change and positioning strategy.

**What you say** is your marketing communications.

**What you do** is your strategic plan.

Those are the most important things you've learned in this entire book. So if your *thinking* isn't there, you will operate aimlessly, and funders won't fund the lack of direction. If your *saying* isn't there, donors won't know about you in the first place. And if your *doing* isn't there, foundations won't see the traction or believe your fundraising pitch.

All three pieces of your brand — thinking, saying, doing — must work harmoniously. Otherwise, you're neither fundable nor findable.

So unite purpose, pitch, and performance. Mindset, message, and movement. Strategy, speech, and steps.

**Be fundable.**

**Be findable.**

**Be unstoppable.**

# Summary.

1. Your brand won't be perfect in the beginning. It's not supposed to be. "Just start and let the work teach you."

2. The cost of most brand mistakes is low, so experiment often. Because brands are 20% psychology and 20% art. But 60% science.

3. Recognition doesn't come from claiming a title (the noun). It comes from taking action (the verb). Often for a long time before anyone notices.

4. A great summary for being fundable and findable is when what you think, what you say, and what you do are in harmony.

5. One last time for those in the back: more fundraising itself can't fix your fundraising. To get funding, be fundable and findable. Brand first, funding second.

# So what do you do next?

### Share these learnings with your team.

Take everything you've learned from this book — hopefully, your notes and highlights and folded pages — and call a leadership team meeting. If your peers have not read the book, give them a copy. Then discuss how you can implement this Fundable/Findable Framework. You have a litany of action steps within each chapter. So start at Chapter 1, assign each action step to a leader, and get to work!

### Recommend this book.

Did you find this book useful? Do you now feel more equipped to be fundable and findable, then able to maximize your funding? It would help others tremendously if you tell another nonprofit leader, or two, or three about Fundable & Findable. Books rely on word-of-mouth to spread. And by spreading this book we can build the social sector field together. So thank you for amplifying this story.

### Review on Amazon and Goodreads.

It would also help tremendously if you leave a review. Amazon and Goodreads are the two main sites where your review will make the most difference. But I'll take any kind words on any platform of your choice!

## Sign up for our online course.

If you need additional help beyond this book, we at Mighty Ally built a self-paced, online course.

You'll be led through dozens of video lessons by me and Founding Partner Eve Wanjiru. Plus you'll get a bonus case study from Founding Partner Kathleen Souder at the end of each module. You'll receive an editable Google Slides copy of all four blueprints you saw in this book (theory of change, strategic plan, positioning strategy, and marketing communications). Not to mention that you'll have access to our course community in the comments, along with free future updates to the course.

Go to mightyally.org/course to learn more.

## Chat to me.

And finally, I'd love to hear how you're getting on with this book — especially, *after* this book. And certainly let me know if you have any feedback or ideas for future revisions. Just email me at kevin@mightyally.org.

Remember, "A book isn't about something; it's for someone."

So thank you for being that someone in this book.

# EPILOGUE

## The unrecognised force fueling the quest for a better world.

By Ingrid Srinath (India)

There is a category of person in the social sector that is labelled "overhead." This group — its size, cost, and growth — are often the subject of hard bargaining between funders and social change organisations.

Of course, we rationally accept that these organisations could not possibly survive or thrive without the people who provide financial management and reporting. Or, those in human resource development and technology support. And — my personal favourites — those fundraisers, campaigners, and brand communications teams. These are the people who raise awareness. They find financial and other resources. They build constituencies of support. And help shape and shift both policy and norms.

This book is an exposition of their work and contribution.

Look around. Everywhere you glance you'll see the impact of these very fundraisers, campaigners, brand and communications folk in our lives. Hospitals, schools and universities, parks, museums, performance venues, places of worship, shelters, soup kitchens, workplace safety, parental leave, vehicle emission standards, vaccines, disaster relief, animal welfare, independent media, medical and scientific research, environmental protection, every major instrument of social welfare, awareness of the climate crisis, attention to the mental health crises, access for people with disabilities, anti-discrimination laws, movements for justice and equity, protection of our most fundamental rights and freedoms, and weekends. Yes, even weekends.

Each of these, and myriad more, owes their existence to some "overhead" individual. Someone raising the resources — in money, skills, social capital, and activism — to make these impacts possible. Yet I seldom see a plaque, statue, or national award dedicated to exponents of this science and art. Even within the social sector, it is founders, innovators, social entrepreneurs, those who deliver services in the field, patrons, and funders who receive the lion's share of accolades. Rarely, if ever, is the spotlight found on the mobilisers of the resources, brand builders, and shapers of perceptions that enable their work.

In fact, all too often, "overhead folk" are the people scapegoated when an organisation fails to achieve its goals. Regardless of where accountability for the gap may vest. These teams rarely have the licence to challenge the purpose, strategies, values, or budgets for which they must find support. This book, thankfully, recognises that these organisational goals and fundraising budgets all begin with clearly defining the brand.

Fundraisers, more than any of their colleagues, must cope with rejection every single day. Too many of their phone calls, emails, letters, and proposals never get so much as a response. The endless quest for meetings and the inordinately long periods of awaiting a decision that too often ends with disappointment. Multiple hoops, often invisible, through which they must jump just to qualify to be selected to receive even relatively small amounts of support. Often pandering to the formidable egos and random whims of funders. All the while begging, nagging, and pestering their colleagues for the information that might help swing a funder's decision in their favour.

Those charged with building and strengthening nonprofit brands must, in addition, face widespread ignorance of the real value of their work. Plus, tremendous reluctance to make the necessary investments — in staffing, attention from organisational leaders, and money. As this book points out, too many organisations see "communications" as a single-person army juggling brand building, fundraising, event management, advocacy campaigns, media relations, and more. Yet almost any activity critical to nonprofit success depends, at least in part, on the strength of the brand.

At a time of seemingly endless conflict, during climate crises that threaten the very survival of our species (especially the most vulnerable among us), runaway inequality, and deeply polarised societies, we are often advised to remember the words of Mr. Rogers, the beloved American TV personality. He once said, "When I was a boy and I would see scary things in the news, my mother would say to me, 'Look for the helpers. You will always find people who are helping.'" Many, if not most, of those helping in the most dire situations are, in fact, fueled by fundraisers, campaigners, and brand-building teams. They are the wind beneath the wings of the countless people working every day to make our world a better place for all.

Picture a world without this formidable force. Ideas that never find fruition. Innovations that never achieve scale. Or art and artists who never find an audience. Talented athletes who never achieve their potential. Diseases whose cures are never discovered or that are delayed by decades. No protection against censorship, surveillance, or unlawful incarceration. Entire swathes of humanity condemned to endless exploitation, exclusion, or worse.

Powered mainly by sheer conviction and resolve, this doughty tribe works tirelessly each day. They persuade us all to take the time and effort necessary to move the needle on every challenge that confronts us as a species. To combat the forces that would return us to brutish times or accelerate the destruction of our planet. To amplify the voices of those who might otherwise never be heard. To permit more of us to enjoy the pleasures of creative expression, whatever form that may take. To preserve the heritage of humanity and to protect our planet and the other species who inhabit it. To strive each day for more just, more equal, more free societies.

We must be grateful not just to these unsung heroes, but also to those who work to help them maximise the outcomes of their effort. And to those who — through research, publication, teaching, and inspiration — enhance the efficiency, effectiveness, and impact of their work. To all those who help unlock the power of technology, behavioural science, and yes, brands, in service of nonprofit fundraising. To the occasional cheerleader who advocates for those who keep our organisational engines fueled. To the leaders of organisations who recognise the need to invest in building knowledge and skills. Those who provide those inputs. And those funders who make the effort to bring a modicum of dignity to the process of resource mobilisation.

To fundraisers, campaigners, brand, and communications folk — take the time to recognise your own value to the organisations and to the multitude of causes that depend on your skills for their viability. Take pride in your accomplishments and celebrate every win. Help your colleagues understand what it takes to achieve success in brand building and fundraising. You could start by taking them through the highlights of this book.

Demand your rightful place in decision-making that determines your outcomes and those of the organisation you serve. Ensure that your leaders know that they own the brand and are its chief custodians. Invest in building your knowledge, skills, and networks to stay abreast of the state of the art. Challenge the power imbalances between funders and the organisations whose work they support. Examine the narratives that you are promoting. About those who have been unjustly treated by our political, social, and economic systems. About those who seek to redress those injustices. And those who provide some of the means to do so.

Delve into every aspect of your brand, and work to craft a brand that fully unleashes the power of your mission. Raise the bar each day for yourself and your colleagues. Connect and build solidarity with fellow "overhead folk" to advance shared norms, standards, and cohesion.

Not just because you deserve it. But because on that recognition rests our collective ability to navigate the daunting challenges confronting humanity and this planet we call home.

# NOTES

"Everything that needs to be said has already been said. But, since no one was listening, everything must be said again."
— André Gide (France)

In this section you'll find detailed notes, references, and citations for each chapter — allowing you to explore these topics further. And for me to give credit where credit is due.

Because "nothing is completely original," says three-time best-selling author Austin Kleon. Creativity is a process of building on the foundation of past work, he continues.

Indeed, we at Mighty Ally have carefully curated and created our Fundable/Findable Framework over the years, thanks to the countless ideas and inspiration from thinkers who came before.

In addition to the exact quotes and in-text references throughout the book, I've listed many sources below. That said, I expect some ideas in this book may be misattributed or a source overlooked. Accidentally, of course. So if you spot any inaccuracies or missed credits, please reach out to me at kevin@mightyally.org so I can address them promptly in future versions.

# Introduction.

[1] The nonprofit starvation cycle is a term that was coined by Ann Goggins Gregory and Don Howard in 2009 in a *Stanford Social Innovation Review* article, called **The Nonprofit Starvation Cycle: Funders must take the lead in breaking a vicious cycle that is leaving nonprofits so hungry for decent infrastructure that they can barely function as organizations — let alone serve their beneficiaries.** In short: the starvation cycle in nonprofits means constant underinvestment in infrastructure — like HR, financial systems, brand communications, and fundraising — to appease low-overhead demands from funders.

[2] **Why More Nonprofits Are Getting Bigger,** Peter Kim and Jeffrey Bradach, The Bridgespan Group (*Stanford Social Innovation Review*, 2012).

[3] **Foundation Assets Are at All-Time Highs, but Don't Expect a Giving Boom,** Sara Herschander (*Chronicle of Philanthropy*, January 4, 2024).

[4] **Nonprofit Impact Matters: How America's Charitable Nonprofits Strengthen Communities and Improve Lives** (National Council of Nonprofits, 2019).

[5] **Half of U.S. Nonprofits at Risk Financially, New Report Shows** (Candid, 2018).

[6] **The Sustainable Development Goals Report 2024** (United Nations, 2024).

[7] **The curious case of the first-time CEO** (Mighty Ally, 2022).

[8] **The Brand IDEA: Managing Nonprofit Brands with Integrity, Democracy, and Affinity,** Nathalie Laidler-Kylander and Julia

Stenzel (2013). This was one of the first books I read, more than a decade ago, when transitioning from the private sector and thinking about how brand applied to nonprofits. This book first introduced me to the bright thinking of Ingrid Srinath (including the quote I used in this introduction), whom I became a fan of and who wrote the epilogue in this very book. I later reference *The Brand IDEA* again in the donor acquisition section. So a huge thanks to both authors for their inspiration and contributions to our field.

# Theory of Change.

[1] **TOC Origins,** The Center for Theory of Change, Inc.

[2] Concept adapted from a tool called **The Climb by Brand the Change,** https://brandthechange.org/blog/free-branding-tool-the-climb-define-your-vision-mission.

[3] **Theory of Change for Brand Communications,** Eve Wanjiru, Acumen Academy, https://acumenacademy.org/course/theory-of-change-brand-communications.

[4] If you want a copy of this full theory of change template (and all the other templates in this book) in editable Google Slides format, sign up for our online course **mightyally.org/course.**

[5] Many of the awesome quotations in this book came directly from beta readers of this book. Through four rounds of beta reading over the course of many months, people from around the world (mostly followers of my content on LinkedIn and Substack) contributed their feedback in the form of commentary. Some of it was so good that I included it directly (with their permission, of course) to diversify the voices and ensure that all the wisdom in this

book didn't just come from best-selling authors you might already know. In addition to this footnote citing the work of Dr. Richard Chivaka, a huge thanks to other beta readers who allowed me to use their quotes: Heather Elisabeth Lanthorn, Dr. Güera Romo, Leonardo Letelier (twice!), Michelle L Christian, Nicole Giuffra, and Marta Lucia de la Cruz Federici.

# 1. The Need.

[1] **How Hardwired Is Human Behavior?**, Nigel Nicholson (*Harvard Business Review*, 1998).

# 2. The Work.

[1] Get more great tools and resources from our friends at **Mulago Foundation** and our own board advisor Kevin Starr, at https://www.mulagofoundation.org/tools.

# 3. The Results.

[1] As I mentioned a few times in the strategic plan section, we at Mighty Ally are big fans of the Entrepreneurial Operating System (EOS®). And we frequently recommend their book **Traction: Get a Grip on Your Business** to our clients, because nobody was really talking about this book in the nonprofit world before we came along. That's why I purposefully honor the EOS model and even use some of their terms in this book, because, as they say, "We like people talking about EOS. We like people using our terms and tools." And they also promise "With that language, we can trust each other at a higher level and solve problems faster. We just ask that when it comes to our language, people give credit where credit is due." Credit given, and thank you!

[2] Jim Collins also took some of the lessons from *Built to Last* and his other popular book, *Good to Great*, and contextualized them for the social sector in **Good to Great and the Social Sectors: Why Business Thinking Is Not the Answer** (2005).

## Strategic Plan.

[1] **Strategy is a verb,** from Delve, is a great read on the topic: https://www.delve.com/insights/strategy-is-a-verb.

[2] Beyond the book *Traction*, highly recommended in the notes above, EOS offers countless free tools at **eosworldwide.com,** plus an official software system at **https://eosone.com.**

[3] **High Score** documentary (Netflix, 2020).

## 4. Team.

[1] My original LinkedIn post on this topic was inspired by and adapted from @thatalliemaison on Twitter/X.

[2] **The AAA Way to Fundraising Success: Maximum Involvement, Maximum Results,** Kay Sprinkel Grace (2009). See more of her books and support her work at https://kaygrace.org.

[3] **Founders of Companies Worth Over a Billion Dollars Have These Simple Things in Common,** Sherin Shibu (*Entrepreneur Magazine*, March 27, 2024).

[4] **Top 5 Reasons Why Nonprofits Fail,** Greg McRay (The Foundation Group, May 28, 2024).

[5] **The curious case of the first-time CEO** (Mighty Ally, 2022).

# 5. Priorities.

[1] I first read about Kongō Gumi in the book **Company of One: Why Staying Small Is the Next Big Thing for Business,** Paul Jarvis (2019).

# 6. Rhythms.

[1] **Business Transformation Ultimate Guide,** Nobl, https://nobl.io/changemaker/business-transformation-ultimate-guide.

# Positioning Strategy.

[1] The phrase "Don't be the best — be the only" is attributed to many people and has become so commonplace that it's hard to tell the original source. But I first read it from Kevin Kelly in his book, **Excellent Advice for Living: Wisdom I Wish I'd Known Earlier** (2023).

[2] Adapted from the Japanese concept of **Ikigai,** the Japanese idea of finding your purpose, rooted in aligning your passions and skills.

[3] If you want a copy of this full positioning strategy template (and all the other templates in this book) in editable Google Slides format, sign up for our online course at **mightyally.org/course.**

[4] Few experts have informed my way of thinking and working better than David C. Baker. While he's an advisor for consulting firms like ours (not nonprofits like yours, alas!), his wisdom can extend to many industries. If you're a thought leader in any field, check out his book **The Business of Expertise: How Entrepreneurial Experts Convert Insight to Impact + Wealth** (2017).

# 7. Landscape.

[1] **3 Benefits of Nonprofit Competition — And Why We Need It,** Tori Utley (*Forbes*, 2018)

[2] The classic **SWOT analysis** is credited, as well as miscredited, to a few people: Albert Humphrey, Robert Franklin Stewart, George Albert Smith Jr., Kenneth Andrews, and C. Roland Christensen. Yes, all white men. Sigh.

# 8. Value Propositions.

[1] Like many of my inspirations, Rick Rubin's great and recent book **The Creative Act: A Way of Being** is not at all related to nonprofits. But for creatives of any sort, it's a must-read.

[2] The original infographic comes from The Bridgespan Group report titled **Funding Strategies of Large US Nonprofits.** The original, full version also includes bonus details on program service fees and investment income, plus examples of nonprofits that fit each funding category.

[3] First invented by **Dave Gray, the creator of Empathy Mapping,** this tool can now be found in countless different versions.

# 9. Brand Personality.

[1] Carl Jung first coined the term "archetypes" in his 1919 essay **Instinct and the Unconscious.** In the past few decades, brand builders increasingly embraced the concept for their organizations. A book that was important to my own understanding of the concept is **The Hero and the Outlaw: Building Extraordinary Brands Through the Power of Archetypes,** Margaret Mark and Carol Pearson (2001).

## Marketing Communications.

[1] **Whistled Languages: Communication and Cybernetics**, René-Guy Busnel and André Classe (1976).

[2] **Typology and acoustic strategies of whistled languages: Phonetic comparison and perceptual cues of whistled vowels** (Cambridge University Press, 2008).

[3] **The Case for Communications** contains an insightful series of articles that reinforce why good communications are critical for nonprofit success, beyond fundraising: https://ssir.org/case_for_communications.

[4] Even with millions of views, it's surprising how many of us still haven't seen this seminal TED Talk, **The way we think about charity is dead wrong:** https://www.ted.com/talks/dan_pallotta_the_way_we_think_about_charity_is_dead_wrong.

[5] **10 Marketing, Web Design & Branding Statistics to Help You Prioritize Business Growth Initiatives,** Gabriel Shaoolian (*Forbes*, 2018).

[6] **Modern Marketing for the Modern Business** (Vermilion Pinstripes).


# 10. Marketing Plan.

[1] While the **PESO Model©** is widely un- and misattributed, it was created by Spin Sucks. Learn more at https://spinsucks.com/the-peso-model.

[2] **The ROI of Email Marketing,** Litmus.

[3] Ross Simmonds is a gold mine of marketing knowledge on social media and in his book, **Create Once, Distribute Forever: How Great Creators Spread Their Ideas and How You Can Too** (2024).

# 11. Messaging & Storytelling.

[1] **Talk Like TED: The 9 Public-Speaking Secrets of the World's Top Minds,** Carmine Gallo (2014).

[2] **The Subconscious Mind of the Consumer (And How To Reach It),** Manda Mahoney (Harvard Business School Working Knowledge, 2003).

[3] **Jerome Bruner,** as cited in an Insight Demand presentation.

[4] **12 Must-Know Stats About Social Media, Fundraising, and Cause Awareness,** Nonprofit Tech for Good (2013).

[5] Marshall Ganz still teaches a course (available to the public) called **Public Narrative: Leadership, Storytelling, and Action** via Harvard Kennedy School Executive Education. Sign up to support his work and learn much more: https://www.hks.harvard.edu/educational-programs/executive-education/public-narrative-leadership-storytelling-and-action.

# 12. Writing & Thought Leadership.

[1] **What to Believe? Impact of Knowledge and Message Length on Neural Activity in Message Credibility Evaluation,** Lukasz Kwasniewicz, Grzegorz M Wojcik, Piotr Schneider, Andrzej Kawiak, Adam Wierzbicki (Frontiers in Human Neuroscience, 2021).

[2] **You Now Have a Shorter Attention Span Than a Goldfish,** Kevin McSpadden (*Time Magazine*, 2015). This data point — first attributed to a study from Microsoft Corp. with researchers in Canada — is the subject of much debate. But I say: who cares if it's eight seconds or 20 seconds or a fish or a cat? We know attention spans are limited.

[3] **Smart Brevity: The Power of Saying More with Less,** Jim VandeHei, Mike Allen, and Roy Schwartz (2022).

[4] **Make Your Point and Get Out of the Way,** Morgan Housel (2017).

[5] **Smart Brevity® 101: How to make your point and have it heard.**

[6] **Bird by Bird: Some Instructions on Writing and Life,** Anne Lamott (1995).

[7] **Write of Passage,** David Perell (2020).

# 13. Visual Identity.

[1] This is according to a hotly debated 3M study done decades ago. Read more at **Research: Is A Picture Worth 1,000 Words Or 60,000 in Marketing,** Matthew Dunn. Regardless of the exact number, it's universally accepted that even a glance at your visuals tells your audience much.

[2] **Information theory — Entropy, Coding, Communication** (Encyclopedia Britannica).

# 14. Pitch Deck.

[1] **The 4 things you need to know about your seed pitch deck,** Russ Heddleston (DocSend 2019).

[2] **Blair Enns, founder of Win Without Pitching,** is also one of my most instrumental career teachers. We weave his firm's sales wisdom into our framework at Mighty Ally, so I mention and reference them a few times in this book. For more, dig into their blog at https://www.winwithoutpitching.com/insights or read their book, **The Win Without Pitching Manifesto.**

[3] **The Science of Effective Presentations** (Prezi).

# 15. Website Strategy.

[1] If you go looking for the Vega Coffee website, unfortunately there isn't one. A few years after our brand engagement, they folded. Why leave them as an example, you ask? First, because many nonprofits and social enterprises are forced to close up shop — we're all attempting the impossible (as in ending poverty and remedying injustice), so we shouldn't be embarrassed about an organizational failure. Second, because it's a good reminder that while a brand can maximize your funding, it's not a panacea. Not a magic wand. Countless other factors (especially leadership) make or break a business or enterprise.

# 16. Corporate Partnerships.

[1] **Shared Value Initiative,** https://www.sharedvalue.org.

[2] We adapted this concept from a mental model we first learned from Justine Blackmore and our friends in corporate partnerships at **Mercy Corps.**

## Donor Acquisition.

[1] This is another phrase that's attributed to many people and has become so commonplace that it's impossible to tell the original source.

## 17. Cultivation.

[1] Adapted from a Naval Ravikant quote: **"If you secretly despise wealth, it will elude you."**

[2] **The E-Myth Revisited: Why Most Small Businesses Don't Work and What to Do About It,** Michael E. Gerber (2004).

[3] I reference and quote **Jeff Brooks** three times in this book because he's that damn good — one of my favorite fundraising writers in the game. Follow his stuff at https://futurefundraisingnow.com for more.

## 18. Solicitation.

[1] **A Guide to Donor Retention,** Bloomerang.

[2] Adapted from the original concept called "The 5 Stages of Awareness" — a copywriting framework popularized by Eugene Schwartz in his book **Breakthrough Advertising** (1966).

[3] I quote **Claire Axelrad, J.D., CFRE** twice in this book, as she's an excellent fundraising thought leader (and coach and consultant) whom you should follow. See her content at https://clairification.com.

[4] **Which story are you telling?** Steven Screen, The Better Fundraising Company (2024).

[5] This is attributed to many people (including Collier Brown, Karl E. Weick, and Adam M. Grant) and has become so commonplace it's impossible to tell the original source.

[6] **Persuasive Business Proposals: Writing to Win More Customers, Clients, and Contracts,** Tom Sant (2012).

# Donor Retention.

[1] **The 15 Biggest NGOs in the World,** Human Rights Careers. https://www.humanrightscareers.com/issues/biggest-ngos-in-the-world.

[2] Data sources: **Association of Fundraising Professionals, Bloomerang, and Mastering Major Gifts.**

# 19. Stewardship.

[1] **Understanding the Reasons for Nonprofit Donor Churn,** Blackbaud (2019).

[2] This truism has been attributed to many people (including Brittany Packnett Cunningham, the Rev. Martin Luther King, Jr., and Jim Wallis). This too has become so commonplace that it's hard to tell the original source.

[3] I quote the fabulous Vu Le twice in this book, reference a book he co-authored, then list him once as a preeminent thought leader once. That's because he is. If you're not following his writings at **NonprofitAF.com,** you're missing out.

## 20. Engagement.

[1] **Don't Diversify Your Nonprofit's Fundraising,** Jamie Bearse (NonprofitPRO 2024).

[2] The Bridgespan Group has published countless resources on this topic, so I recommend that you look into its original study, **How Nonprofits Get Really Big** (*Stanford Social Innovation Review*, 2007); **Why More Nonprofits Are Getting Bigger** (*Stanford Social Innovation Review*, 2012); plus **A New Look at How US Nonprofits Get Really Big** (*Stanford Social Innovation Review*, 2024).

[3] **Nonprofit Challenges: What Foundations Can Do,** Ellie Buteau, Ph.D., Andrea Brock, and Mark Chaffin (The Center for Effective Philanthropy, 2013).

[4] **Unicorns Unite: How Nonprofits & Foundations Can Build Epic Partnerships,** Jane Leu, Jessamyn Shams-Lau, and Vu Le (2018).

[5] **How Effective Partnerships With Foundations Can Transform Your Nonprofit** (Fox Grants, 2024)

## Conclusion.

[1] This is just an estimate, from me. I'll do a randomized controlled trial one day to prove it.

[2] The famous Silicon Valley expression, **"If you are not embarrassed by the first version of your product, you've launched too late,"** has largely been attributed to Reid Hoffman, the founder of LinkedIn.

[3] It comes from a 1997 Clint Black song titled **Something That We Do,** if you really must know.

# ABOUT THE AUTHOR

"The two most important days in your life are the day you are born and the day you find out why." — Mark Twain (United States)

Kevin L. Brown is a writer, a speaker, and CEO of the nonprofit hybrid Mighty Ally. He initially spent 15 years building private sector brands. From Apple to Adidas, Formula One to fintech startups. And in his first four corporate gigs, Kevin helped each company scale towards acquisition, including one he co-founded.

Then, a passion for the orphan crisis (his *why*) led to living in Uganda, followed by South Africa, Mauritius, and Malaysia. In 2017, he co-founded Mighty Ally — Uganda's second-ever B Corp.

Kevin is an Acumen East Africa Fellow, plus an advisor for two grantmakers: Roddenberry Foundation and Greenwood Place. He served on the board of Impact Hub, won a Valiente Award at SXSW and a NEXT Award for Startup of the Year, was named an Executive Influencer by Billboard Magazine, and proudly sports a torn Achilles from the Ironman World Championship.

Three daughters from Uganda and China fuel his work to end poverty and injustice. Years ago, he and his high-school sweetheart wife sold their house, car, and everything they owned. And they set out as a nomadic family of five — with only a backpack and suitcase each — to live on every continent together by 2030.

# ABOUT MIGHTY ALLY

"As long as poverty, injustice, and gross inequality persist in our world, none of us can truly rest." — Nelson Mandela (South Africa)

Mighty Ally is a nonprofit hybrid — fighting poverty and injustice in lockstep with our clients. Founded in 2017 between Uganda and the United States, we guide courageous nonprofit leaders to be fundable and findable.

Our Fundable/Findable Framework is a way to simplify and demystify the concept of brand. And we have an unmatched international perspective for a purposefully small team, with Global North and South co-founders. Plus hundreds of clients in dozens of countries across six continents.

We're a catalyst between grantees and grantmakers — sparking insights and understanding by guiding both sides as clients. And we focus exclusively on the growth and early stage.

Our leadership team has founded, run, or turned around six small businesses. We started our careers in the private sector, spending decades working on the world's most iconic brands. Now we favor the underdogs.

Brand first, funding second.

# ABOUT THE ILLUSTRATOR

"Art should comfort the disturbed and disturb the comfortable." — Banksy (England)

Michelle Benson is the Founder of Culture of Philanthropy, an organization that trains fundraisers, CEOs, communication teams, and consultants worldwide to "be found" by high-value funders on LinkedIn.

Michelle combines her coaching expertise with her ability to craft illustrations that capture the heart of fundraising, to be "found" herself. Her first 100 graphics posted on LinkedIn amassed 5.3 million impressions, gaining her 30,000 new followers and hundreds of nonprofits signing up to work with her.

Dedicated to helping nonprofits stand out and get funded, Michelle was the perfect choice to illustrate this book.

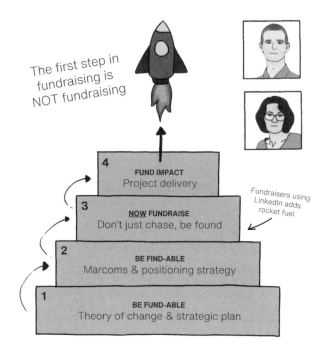

FIGURE 33: The original illustration that started the Benson/Brown collaboration.

# ACKNOWLEDGMENTS

"When you drink water, remember the source." — Vietnamese proverb

Sure, saying that *this book wouldn't exist without you* is a cliché. But clichés exist for a reason. So this isn't just a list of acknowledgments. It's a spotlight on the people who made Fundable & Findable possible.

Huge thanks to:

**My Founding Partners at Mighty Ally.** Kathleen Souder (my work sister) for a decade of thought partnership, a lifetime of social justice advocacy, and years of helping shape this Fundable/Findable Framework. Eve Wanjiru for being such a lovely human to work with, creating the "other side" of our business we didn't even know we were missing, and bringing the passion to serve those who are unseen, unheard, and underfunded. And Sarah Callaway Brown for serving as my creative collaborator on every single book decision big and small, editing this manuscript three times front to back, holding down the fort (Wayne) during my four writing retreats, and (most importantly) for being my personal steady as I navigated all the emotional up-and-downs that came with being a first-time author — you were truly the copilot of this book.

**Our Mighty Ally team, clients, and allies.** 340 clients in 51 countries so far, including funding partners like Cartier Philanthropy, Dovetail Impact Foundation, Roddenberry Foundation, Pace Able Foundation, and more. The 100+ different people and agencies who have helped us serve our clients since 2017. Nonprofit board members Tim Rann and Jonathan Wright for being on this journey with us since day one. Board advisors both then and now, like Sharath Jeevan for sharing initial insights about book writing and Barak Bruerd for guidance in the early years. Our first-ever clients, Ash Rogers and Julius Mbeya at Lwala Community Alliance, for giving this startup a chance, then being consummate ambassadors for our work.

**Book contributors.** Michelle Benson for her camaraderie that helped keep social media algorithms from crushing my very soul, and — along with Belle! — for the incredible illustrations in this book. Ingrid Srinath for her book interview, wisdom she brings to our sector, the beautiful epilogue she wrote for this book, and her ongoing partnership. Danielle Goodman for providing the much-needed substantive edits and initial guidance. Mark Woodworth and Editcetera for the excellent copyediting. Ameesha, Niall, Kyle, and the full team at The Book Shelf for the cover/interior design, proofreading, marketing, and publishing support. Katherine at Red Press Publishing who was the first professional I spoke to about this project, giving me some incredibly useful feedback on the structure and introduction. Russ Smith for his year of pixel-perfect brand work like the book landing page. And to two authors whom I've never met but whose books tremendously helped me in this journey: AJ Harper (*Write a Must-Read*) and Rob Fitzpatrick (*Write Useful Books*).

**Reader interviews and beta readers.** Camila Jordan, Jena Nardella, John Nyagwencha, Kendra Jeffreys, Victor Odhiambo, Kushal Chakravorty, and Nivi Sharma for being among the first people I interviewed about this book. Then all the 273 people in 49 countries below for being beta readers and supporters (a special thanks to Güera, Mark, Heather, Angela, Christina, Justine, Damian, Kira-Leigh, Leizl, Michelle, Nicole, Stephanie, Marta Lucia, and others for going over and beyond to not just read and comment, but provide the extra feedback and support). Beta readers and ambassadors include A.K.M Bulbul Ahmed, Abdullahi D. Hassan, Adinor Puplampu, Adriana Alejandro Osorio, Alba Carrasco Perez, Alex Knezovich, Alex Parks, Alexa White, Alexandra Mandelbaum, Alina Nosenko, Amar Kharate, Amelia Pruchnicki, Amenze (Iyoha) Eguavoen, Ana Ligia Scachetti, Andrea Dickson, Andrew Thorburn, Angela Wier, Angi Yoder-Maina, Ph.D., Annastacia Kuria, Anne Rweyora K., Antonella Abategiovanni, Aradhana Gurung, Aron Halevi, Arun Kumar, Audrey Relut, Awuor Ayiecho, Aye Kyithar Swe, Ayushi Bhati, Balkrishna "BK" Korgaonkar, Bernardo Garrido, Bilal Attal, Bill Duffy, Boris Martin, Brenda Asiimwe, Brian Greenwald, Brittany Cesarini, Busang Maruping, Cameron Parry, Camila Jordan, Carl Atiya Swanson, Carla Birnberg, Carla Perdiz, Carla W., Charles A., Charlotte Wilmot, Chris Martin, Christina Berry-Moorcroft, Christina Stanton, Clara Radhakrishna, Claudia Shilumani, Clea Strydom, Cowan Koduk, Cristina López, Cynthia Betti, Damian Chapman, Danami-Maurice Champion, Dani Saraiva, Daniel Shaffer, Daniela Cunha, Daniela Weiers, David N. Kaguima, David Sturmes-Verbeek, Davide Tamburlini, Deborah Maufi MD, Dexter Sam, Dritan Shala, Eduardo Monge, Elisabeth von Ketteler, Elizabeth Joseph, Elsi Rizvanolli, Erin Donley Marineau,

Esa Dwiyan, Esther Amunga, Eva Cruz, Evelyn Nassuna, Faith (Wangari) Kinyanjui, Farah Sofa, Giovanna Tanzi, Godwin A. Bamsa, Guadalupe Mendoza Trejo, Güera Romo, Gul Dawlatyan, Gustav Appiah, Hamsini Ravi, Harafik Harafik, Heather Elisabeth Lanthorn, Heidi Albert, Hermela Alemneh, Hezron (Karinga) Karanja, Indu Sambandam, Inés Lambertini, Innocent (Olur) Ociti, Izabela (Iza) de Souza, J.Paul Fridenmaker, Jackie Johnston, Jackson Cooper, James Williams, Jamie Johnson, Jane Ordaz Stubbs, Jane Porter, Janet Mitton, Jankiel Rosenwald Wulff, Jarrett Collins, Jennifer Barrette Trainor, Jenny Löfbom, Jeremiah Kuria, Jeremy P. Barker, Jerome Scriptunas, Jodi Henderson, Joe Kirkenir, Joseph Katsala, Josephine Akia, Josh Goralski, Josh Guenther, Judith Madigan, Juliett Achieng' Otieno, Justine Miley, Katherine Ko, Katia Lord, Katja Schiller Nwator, Katrina Hosie, Keicy Cabrera, Kellie Wishart, Kelly Byers, Khalid Bakali, Kim Langbecker, Kira-Leigh Kuhnert, Kirsty Kaiser, Kristy Payne, Kushal Agarwal, Laura Vitto, Leigh (Juries) Swartz, Leila Aly El Deen, Leizl Eykelhof, Leonardo Letelier, Leonardo Saraiva, Lesley-Anne Long, Linda Corkery, Linda Jones, Lisa Chensvold, Lisa Quinn, Lucy Ruiz, Luke Wilkinson, Ly Tran, Lynn Stanier, Lynne Viccaro O'Leary, Mahlet S Bekele, Mahmoud Khatib, Malcolm Mooi, Malgorzata (Margaret) Bryndal, Manivanh Khy, Mara Renn, Marcelo Zenga, Marcia Felth, Mardie Torres, Margaret Heighton, Maria O. Alvarez, Mariana Morais Sarmento, Marilyn Cosola, Mark Dombkins, Marta Lucia de la Cruz Federici, Maryna Ryzhkova, Matthew Osborne-Smith, Matthew Wilson, Maya (Reagan) Di Bello, Mayford Manika, Mena Kalokoh, Michael Bäcklund, Michelle Gollapalli, Michelle L. Christian, Miriam Wachira, Monika Halsan, Muthoni Thuo, Mutlu Yetkin, Mutuna Chanda, Myles Delfin, Nagesh N. Borse, Natalia Pinzon Granados, Natalie Haigh, Natasha Mulenga Hornsby, Neer Rao, Neeru Chaudhary, Nelvin Johnson, Nicole Giuffra, Niki Fredrick,

Nikki Fisher, Nivi Sharma, Olanrewaju Oniyitan, Olga Maximova, Pankaja Balaji, Patience Finye Andrew, Patricia Del Claro, Patricia Gyan-Bassaw, Paul Semeh, Paul Sternberg, Peirong Lin, Peter Olakunle Adeeko, Pius Isabirye, Pramita Saha, Prashant Mehra, Purva Gupta, Rafael Medeiros, Ravi S K, Razali (Raz) Samsudin, Rebecca Stutsman, Rebecca Zeigler Mano, Remy Kalter, Richard Chivaka, RN Mohanty, Robert Nolan, Rodrigo Pipponzi, Rosetta M., Roule le Roux, Ryan le Roux, Sabeena Mathayas, Samuel Ozonna, Sandhya C. Rao, Sarah Bogg, Scott Revo, Selim Uysal, Seth Cochran, Seth Mulli, Shalini Kapoor, Shekar Hariharan, Shelly Satuku, Shep Owen, Shirine (Bakhat) Pont, Shounak Pande, Shruti Patel, Sietske Broekhuizen, Simon Balemba Effansa, Sonia Buma, Sophie Olivier, Stella Nankya, Stephanie Starling, Steve Wanta, Subhadip Bhattacharya, Sumayiya Nanyonjo, Sunil Lalvani, Susie Brook, Sweeha Panwar, Syed Abrar Rehmani, Tamar Messer, Temi Okubadejo, Tharcisse Nshimirimana, Theresa-Danielle Hamilton, Thomas Lewis, Tinacho Gerald Chitongo, Tom Daniels, Tracy Culleton, Twesigye Jackson Kaguri, Ugochi Obidiegwu, Vadette Radford, Valerie Guerin, Venu Gupta, Vera Penêda, Victor Odhiambo, Virginia Tarozzi, Willson Chivhanga, Xoli Fuyani, Yahuza Hambali, Zoe Smith.

**LinkedIn and Substack community.** The more than 85,000 followers and subscribers — many of whom I feel like I know, despite us having never met or spoken — for the constant support via comments, reposts, likes, direct messages, and amplification of this content. Your kind words are like fuel to keep writing.

**My family.** My mother for taking me to that summer writing workshop when I was 10 (which inspired me to be an author), for her unwavering commitment to this family despite what wild thing we're up to next that she might not fully like or agree with (but always finds a way to support), and for no doubt reading this book word for word because that's how she loves. My father for being a rabid reader while I was growing up (with 25 books and magazines always piled up beside the chair) and for giving me my first glimpse of entrepreneurship. My brother for being the best friend and the best Shu Shu my kids could ever dream of, and reminding me — via various 48-hour visits in various countries — not to take life *too* seriously. Enock (the son I never had, but do now) for keeping the house afloat during that messy startup phase of Mighty Ally, then supporting my LinkedIn content and learning to be an excellent nonprofit communicator along the way. Dabo for keeping a book in her face and inspiring me to be a better author. Junebug for being the creative light in any room and inspiring me to think outside the box. And Meebs for her sweet, patient spirit and inspiring me to have more grace. (Remember rascals: The Browns don't give up!)

**And lastly, Goose, only because she deserves the final word.** My first love, my only love, my soulmate forever. It's an embarrassment of riches for a brute like me to have a beautiful and talented partner like you, in both work and life. You are the most versatile, well-rounded human I've ever known. And I pinch myself that you picked me to do life with. I pick you too, Goose.

# PRAISE FOR THE BOOK

"A brand is no longer what we tell the consumer it is; it is what consumers tell each other it is." — Scott Cook

"*Fundable & Findable demystifies, democratises, and delights.*" — Dr. Stephanie S. Starling (England)

"*Finally a Bible for nonprofit leaders by someone who knows the pains and the opportunities of fundraising well.*" — Kassaga Arinaitwe (Uganda)

"*Don't know how to talk about your organization? Do what Kevin L. Brown says. That's all.*" — Anne Hager (United States)

"*Fundable & Findable resonates so deeply. It's practical, doable, and builds on intuition and empathy.*" — Ratna Viswanathan (India)

"*You are truly the Robin Hood of our international development arena.*" — Cheikh Eteka Traore (Nigeria)

*"Es uno de los libros más útiles, si no el más útil, debido a la generosidad de toda la información, fuentes, herramientas y guía paso a paso."* — Marta Lucia de la Cruz Federici (Colombia)

*"Kevin L. Brown is the next generation Dan Pallotta."* — Josh Goralski (United States)

*"This book about the challenges of running a nonprofit is so affirming. I feel seen. It inspires me to keep striving to make a better world."* — Thea Stinear (Australia)

*"The advice is concrete, crisp, and fun to read. So many organizations keep looking for magic, quick-fix formulas for fundraising. Kevin makes it clear that there is magic, but it's never quick. Do yourself a favor and read this book."* — Jo Chopra-McGowan (India)

*"There are few people who have a mastery of fundraising concepts like Kevin L. Brown."* — Tracy Ballot, CFRE (United States)

*"We have transformed our brand, visioning, and fundraising system because of this book."* — John Jal Dak (Uganda)

"As a neurodiverse founder of a nonprofit who doesn't come from a corporate/finance background, the amount of funding information at first was completely overwhelming. This book makes it more digestible." — Ryan Burlak (Australia)

"This book is a lighthouse for many." — Kushal Chakravorty (India)

"Fundable & Findable gives simple and direct ways to get nonprofits out of our heads and out of our own ways when it comes to building a brand and raising money." — Rakiba Kibria (United States)

"Wish the world has more of you Kevin L. Brown. You are truly a brave soul, a beacon and a voice for the voiceless." — Wilton Otto (Canada)

"We have received a gift of $8 million from MacKenzie Scott. And we have built a bold strategy where we are going to invest in branding, fundraising, training, diversity and inclusion, co-funding, partners, and so many other important things that we could not afford to do before. This book was essential to these decisions." — Cynthia Betti (Brazil)

*"Fundable & Findable had a positive impact on my communication approach with funders, sponsors, and volunteers. I have transitioned to a storytelling method that incorporates concise data, yielding successful results." —* Raymond Amezado (Ghana)

*"Want more funding for your mission? Read this book."* — Natalie Rekstad (United States)